Reading for Understanding

Toward a R&D Program
in Reading Comprehension

RAND Reading Study Group
Catherine Snow, Chair

Prepared for the
**Office of Educational Research
and Improvement (OERI)**

Science & Technology Policy Institute | **RAND**
EDUCATION

The research described in this report was prepared for the Office of Educational Research and Improvement (OERI), U.S. Department of Education.

Library of Congress Cataloging-in-Publication Data

Snow, Catherine E.
    Reading for understanding : toward a research and development program in reading comprehension / Catherine Snow.
      p. cm.
    "MR-1465."
    Includes bibliographical references.
    ISBN 0-8330-3105-8
    1. Reading comprehension—Research. 2. Reading—Research. I. Title.

LB1050.45 .S57 2002
428.4'3—dc21

2001048905

RAND is a nonprofit institution that helps improve policy and decisionmaking through research and analysis. RAND® is a registered trademark. RAND's publications do not necessarily reflect the opinions or policies of its research sponsors.

Cover designed by Barbara Angell Caslon

Published 2002 by RAND
1700 Main Street, P.O. Box 2138, Santa Monica, CA 90407-2138
1200 South Hayes Street, Arlington, VA 22202-5050
201 North Craig Street, Suite 102, Pittsburgh, PA 15213-1516
RAND URL: http://www.rand.org/
To order RAND documents or to obtain additional information, contact
Distribution Services: Telephone: (310) 451-7002; Fax: (310) 451-6915; Email:
order@rand.org

One of the most vexing problems facing middle and secondary school teachers today is that many students come into their classrooms without the requisite knowledge, skills, or disposition to read and comprehend the materials placed before them. In an effort to inform the U.S. Department of Education's Office of Educational Research and Improvement (OERI) on ways to improve the quality and relevance of education research and development, RAND convened 14 experts with a wide range of disciplinary and methodological perspectives in the field of reading. The RAND Reading Study Group (RRSG) was charged with proposing strategic guidelines for a long-term research and development program supporting the improvement of reading comprehension. This report is the product of that group's efforts and of the valuable commentary provided by various members of the reading research and practice communities.

This report should be of interest to those involved with the planning of education research and development (R&D) programs by public and private agencies, and it should also be of interest to researchers who study reading instruction and practitioners who teach reading.

This report is the first in a series of three RAND reports dealing with the topic of education R&D. The second report, scheduled for draft publication in summer 2002, will propose an R&D program for mathematics education and the third report, scheduled for draft publication in fall 2002, will address R&D management issues.

Funding for the RRSG research was provided under a contract with OERI. The research was carried out under the auspices of RAND Education and the Science and Technology Policy Institute (S&TPI), a federally funded research and development center sponsored by the National Science Foundation and managed by RAND.

Inquiries regarding RAND Education and the S&TPI may be directed to the following individuals:

Helga Rippen, Director
Science and Technology Policy Institute
RAND, 1200 South Hayes Street
Arlington, VA 22202-5050
(703) 413-1100 x5351
Email: stpi@rand.org

Dominic Brewer, Director
RAND Education
RAND, 1700 Main Street
Santa Monica, CA 90407-2138
(310) 393-0411 x7515
Email: education@rand.org

CONTENTS

FIGURES

TABLES

Recent research on reading instruction has led to significant improvements in the knowledge base for teaching primary-grade readers and for ensuring that those children have the early-childhood experiences they need to be prepared for the reading instruction they receive when they enter school. Nevertheless, evidence-based improvements in the teaching practices of reading comprehension are sorely needed. Understanding how to improve reading comprehension outcomes, not just for students who are failing in the later grades but for all students who are facing increasing academic challenges, should be the primary motivating factor in any future literacy research agenda.

In 1999, the Office of Educational Research and Improvement of the U.S. Department of Education charged the RAND Reading Study Group (RRSG) with developing a research agenda to address the most-pressing issues in literacy. The decision to focus this research agenda proposal on reading comprehension in particular was motivated by a number of factors:

- All high school graduates are facing an increased need for a high degree of literacy, including the capacity to comprehend complex texts, but comprehension outcomes are not improving.

- Students in the United States are performing increasingly poorly in comparison with students in other countries as they enter the later years of schooling when discipline-specific content and subject-matter learning are central to the curriculum.

- Unacceptable gaps in reading performance persist between children in different demographic groups despite the efforts over recent decades to close those gaps; the growing diversity of the U.S. population will likely widen those gaps even further.

- Little direct attention has been devoted to helping teachers develop the skills they need to promote reading comprehension, ensure content learning through reading, and deal with the differences in comprehension skills that their students display.

- Policies and programs (e.g., high-stakes testing, subject-related teacher credentialing, literacy interventions) intended to improve reading comprehension are regularly adopted, but their effects are uncertain because the programs are neither based on empirical evidence nor adequately evaluated.

The RRSG believes that a vigorous, cumulative research and development program focused on reading comprehension is essential if the nation is to address these education problems successfully. Current research and development efforts have been helpful in addressing such problems, but those efforts are limited in their funding, unsystematic in their pursuit of knowledge and improved teaching practice, and neglectful of strategies for taking evidence-based practices to scale.

The program of reading research that the RRSG is proposing fits into the larger context of research on reading in the United States. The Interagency Education Research Initiative—funded jointly by the National Science Foundation, OERI, and the National Institute of Child Health and Human Development—is sponsoring efforts that bring early research to scale with some emphasis on the use of technology. Thus, the reading research program proposed by the RRSG seeks to fill any gaps left by the existing research efforts, while being coherently organized around a central set of issues facing practitioners.[1]

In this report, the RRSG characterizes reading comprehension in a way that the group believes will help organize research and development activities in the domain of reading comprehension. This characterization builds on the current knowledge base on reading comprehension, which is sizeable but sketchy, unfocused, and inadequate as a basis for reform in reading comprehension instruction. Research has shown that many children who read at the third-grade level in grade 3 will not automatically become proficient comprehenders in later grades. Therefore, teachers must teach comprehension explicitly, beginning in the primary grades and continuing through high school. Research has also shown that a teacher's expertise makes a big difference in this effort; yet, few teachers receive adequate pre-service preparation or ongoing professional development focused on reading comprehension. Finally, research has also shown that improving reading comprehension and preventing poor reading outcomes require measuring outcomes at every stage of learning.

---

[1]The term *practitioners* in this report refers to all school district staff, including teachers, principals, and district administrators and also tutors and any other individuals implementing education as opposed to conducting research on it.

Therefore, the RRSG proposes three specific *domains* as having the highest priority for further research: instruction, teacher preparation, and assessment. In making this proposal, the RRSG emphasizes the need for research that builds on previous research findings about reading comprehension, contributes to better theories of reading development, and produces knowledge that is usable in both classrooms and policymaking arenas.

Within the federal agencies that are collectively responsible for carrying out research and development related to literacy, the capability to plan, manage, and execute the program envisioned by the RRSG is not well developed. This is particularly true within the Office of Education Research and Improvement (OERI), the agency that has the clearest mandate for addressing the problems outlined in this report. Thus, in addition to suggesting a structure and broad priorities for a program of research, the RRSG also suggests principles that might improve the management of the program.

A HEURISTIC FOR THINKING ABOUT READING COMPREHENSION

Learning to read well is a long-term developmental process. At the end point, the proficient adult reader can read a variety of materials with ease and interest, can read for varying purposes, and can read with comprehension even when the material is neither easy to understand nor intrinsically interesting. The RRSG's thinking about reading comprehension was informed by a vision of proficient readers who are capable of acquiring new knowledge and understanding new concepts, are capable of applying textual information appropriately, and are capable of being engaged in the reading process and reflecting on what is being read.

The RRSG began its thinking by defining the term *reading comprehension* as the process of simultaneously extracting and constructing meaning through interaction and involvement with written language. It consists of three elements: the reader, the text, and the activity or purpose for reading. The RRSG developed a heuristic to show how these elements interrelate in reading comprehension, an interrelationship that occurs within a larger sociocultural context that shapes and is shaped by the reader and that interacts with each of the elements iteratively throughout the process of reading. This idea is illustrated in Figure S.1.

The Reader

The reader brings to the act of reading his or her cognitive capabilities (attention, memory, critical analytic ability, inferencing, visualization); motivation (a purpose for reading, interest in the content, self-efficacy as a reader);

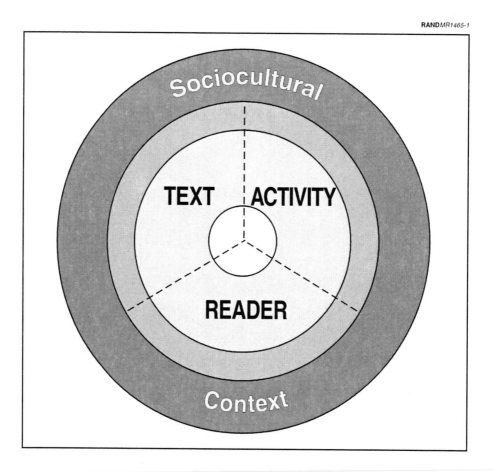

Figure S.1— A Heuristic for Thinking About Reading Comprehension

knowledge (vocabulary and topic knowledge, linguistic and discourse knowledge, knowledge of comprehension strategies); and experiences.

These attributes vary considerably among readers (inter-individual differences)
and vary even within an individual reader as a function of the particular text
and activity (intra-individual differences). Although considerable research has
shown that each of these attributes relates to comprehension outcomes, the
education field knows very little about how to most effectively enhance those
attributes instructionally. Nor does the education field know how to limit the
particular challenges that second-language readers face due to those readers'
limited vocabulary and linguistic knowledge, nor do educators know how to
build on those readers' first-language comprehension abilities.

The Text

The features of any given text have a large impact on comprehension. While reading, the reader constructs various representations of the text that are important for comprehension. Those representations include the *surface code* (the exact wording of the text), the *text base* (idea units representing the meaning of the text), and the *mental models* (the way in which information is processed for meaning) that are embedded in the text. Electronic text presents particular challenges to comprehension (e.g., dealing with the non-linear nature of hypertext), but it also offers the potential to support comprehension by providing hyperlinks to definitions of difficult words or other supplementary material.

Thirty years ago, children were assigned specific readings that were crafted for instructional purposes, or they were exposed to a select group of books in the narrative, descriptive, expository, or persuasive genres. We now live in a society that is experiencing an explosion of alternative texts that vary widely in content, reading levels, and genre. These texts incorporate multimedia and electronic options and are geared to a variety of cultures and groups. The sheer volume of reading choices makes it much more difficult for teachers to select appropriate texts for individual readers. Research that would identify reader capabilities and limitations more precisely and that would chart the impact of different text features on readers with varying capabilities would offer teachers considerable help in understanding the reading comprehension phenomenon.

The Activity

The reading activity involves one or more purposes or tasks, some operations to process the text, and the outcomes of performing the activity, all of which occur within some specific context. The initial purpose for the activity can change as the reader reads. That is, a reader may encounter information that raises new questions and makes the original purpose insufficient or irrelevant. Processing the text involves decoding the text, higher-level linguistic and semantic processing, and self-monitoring for comprehension—all of which depend on reader capabilities as well as on the various text features. Each element of text processing has varying degrees of importance depending on the type of reading being done, such as skimming (getting the gist of the text) or studying (reading the text with the intent of retaining the information for a period of time). Finally, the outcomes of reading are part of the activity. The outcomes can include an increase in knowledge, a solution to some real-world problem, and/or engagement with the text. However, these outcomes may or may not map directly to the reader's initial purpose in reading.

The long-term outcomes of reading—improved reading comprehension ability, increased knowledge, and engagement with the text—are of the greatest direct relevance to educators. One of the nation's highest priorities should be to define the instructional practices that generate long-term improvements in learners' comprehension capacities and thus promote learning across content areas.

The Context

When one thinks of the context in which reading is taught, the first thing that comes to mind is the classroom. But the learning process for reading takes place within a context that extends far beyond the classroom. In fact, differences among readers can, to some extent, be traced to the varying sociocultural environments in which children live and learn to read. Learning and literacy are viewed partly as cultural and historical activities, not just because they are acquired through social interactions but also because they represent how a specific cultural group or discourse community interprets the world and transmits information. If the education community is to ensure universal success in reading comprehension, those in the community must understand the full range of sociocultural differences in communicative practices. Sociocultural differences are often correlated with group differences. Groups may be identified by income, race, ethnicity, native language, or neighborhood. Substantial research considers group membership apart from sociocultural differences, but further research is needed regarding the relationship between membership in certain groups and reading comprehension.

ELEMENTS OF A RESEARCH AND DEVELOPMENT PROGRAM

The need for research in reading comprehension is critical and the possibilities for research topics in this area are nearly endless. The mission of improving reading comprehension outcomes is too important to leave to laissez-faire research managers. The research community needs to set an agenda that defines the most serious problems and prioritizes the needed research.

The RRSG has made recommendations for a research agenda and developed criteria for prioritizing the potential projects and evaluating proposals. First and foremost, the research should yield knowledge that is practical and usable in classrooms and in guiding educational policy. A potential project should be judged not only by its methodological rigor but also by its capacity to generate improvements in classroom practices, enhance curricula, enrich teacher preparation, and produce more-informative assessments of reading comprehension.

A research program that incorporates a range of quantitative and qualitative methodologies is essential to ensure rigor in answering the research questions and to generate practical and useful knowledge.

Projects should build on existing research when possible. For example, a substantial body of existing research about the development of word reading among primary-age children has contributed to successful interventions for children who experience difficulties in reading. Clearly, the reading-outcomes benefits that accrue from improved instruction in word reading will be limited if children do not also have access to improved instruction in vocabulary, oral language production, writing, text analysis, and other high-level operations that contribute to comprehension.

An educational research program must address widespread doubts concerning the quality, relevance, and usability of educational research. High-quality research efforts should be long-term and cumulative. And we as researchers should create links across the now-distinct subfields and subgroups of research in this field. One way to reach this goal is through well-designed proposal-review procedures that contribute to the task of forming a community of researchers linked by their common intellectual focus. Collaboration also provides a healthy forum for quality control and the judicious use of resources.

In drafting an agenda for a research and development program, the RRSG outlined key research questions that should be addressed within each of the three high-priority domains of comprehension research—instruction, teacher preparation, and assessment.

An Agenda for Research on Reading Instruction

Good instruction is the most powerful means of promoting the development of proficient comprehenders and preventing reading comprehension problems. A good teacher makes use of practices that employ his or her knowledge about the complex and fluid interrelationships among readers, texts, purposeful activities, and contexts to advance students' thoughtful, competent, and motivated reading. Instructional research must acknowledge the complexity of these interrelationships if it is to generate knowledge that is usable in real-life classrooms.

Given what is already known about how students learn to read and reading instruction, the RRSG identified some urgent questions related to reading instruction that need to be answered, such as:

- Would simply increasing the amount of time devoted to comprehension instruction while continuing to use practices that are currently in place improve outcomes?

- How does the teaching community ensure that all children have the vocabulary and background knowledge they need to comprehend certain content areas and advanced texts?

- How can excellent, direct comprehension instruction be embedded into content instruction that uses inquiry-based methods and authentic reading materials?

- How do national, state, and local policies and practices facilitate or impede the efforts of teachers to implement effective comprehension instruction?

Teacher Preparation and Professional Development in Reading Comprehension

Regardless of the quantity and quality of research-based knowledge about comprehension, students' reading achievement will not improve unless teachers use that knowledge to improve their instruction. There is a good reason to look closely at this issue: Researchers find that most teachers, even those who say they use reform models, still rely primarily on traditional practices. Other researchers point to the importance of teacher quality as a critical variable in student achievement.

In this report, the RRSG has provided a few ideas about how to enlist teachers to support reform efforts, how to enhance their capacity to contribute to reform efforts, and how to engage them in reshaping reform efforts in response to their experiences with enacting reform. The RRSG believes that teachers must be front and center in discussions about how to improve comprehension instruction in schools today.

Research has shown that well-designed teacher preparation programs have a positive effect on reading outcomes. But some critical questions have not been answered by the research. For example:

- What knowledge base (e.g., regarding language development, sociolinguistics, multiculturalism, reading development) do teachers need to provide effective reading comprehension instruction?

- What is the relative power of various instructional delivery systems (e.g., field-based experiences, video-based cases, demonstration teaching, microteaching) for helping teachers acquire the knowledge and skills they need to successfully teach comprehension with students of different ages and in different contexts?

We know that the expertise of the teacher matters a lot to reading instruction outcomes, but several questions still need to be addressed in the area of teacher expertise. For example:

- What content (declarative and procedural knowledge about readers, text, tasks, and contexts) and sequencing of content are present in effective professional development programs?

- What are the critical components of professional development that lead to effective instruction and sustained change in teachers' practices?

Assessment of Reading Comprehension

All of the research recommended by the RRSG depends on having better instruments for assessing reading comprehension. The impact of assessment on instruction constitutes a research agenda of its own, particularly in the current era of accountability-oriented education reform. A system of reading comprehension assessment should reflect the full array of important comprehension outcomes and a research program should establish appropriate levels of performance for children of different ages and grades based on those outcomes. Without research-based benchmarks defining adequate progress in comprehension, we as a society risk aiming far too low in our expectations for student learning.

The RRSG proposes an approach to assessment that differs from current approaches in that it is based on an appropriately rich and elaborated theory of reading comprehension. The assessment procedures in this approach will be fluid, and they will change as more is learned from the research. More value will be placed on their usefulness for improving instruction. And because comprehensive assessment systems can place significant time demands on students and teachers, the education community has an obligation to develop assessments that are an integral part of and supportive of instruction, rather than limited to serving the needs of researchers.

Teachers who are interested in improving their instruction need reliable and valid assessments that are closely tied to their curricula so that they can identify those students who are learning and those who need extra help. The comprehension assessments that are widely used today focus heavily on only a few tasks and thus may inadvertently limit the reading curriculum to preparation for those few tasks. Knowledge, application, and engagement are all critical outcomes of reading with comprehension; assessments that reflect all three of these outcomes are needed.

Several key questions about assessment follow: Given this analysis, two important questions about assessment need to be answered:

- What would it take to design valid and reliable measures of student self-regulated strategic reading that teachers can administer in the classroom to inform their instructional decisions and to identify children who may need additional instruction?

- What would it take to design measures of reading comprehension that are sensitive to instructional interventions as well as to specific forms of reading instruction for all readers?

RECOMMENDED IMPROVEMENTS TO MAKE THE PROPOSED RESEARCH PROGRAM FEASIBLE

For the RRSG's proposed research program to develop to the point that it can actually improve comprehension outcomes, the research program infrastructure will need to be improved in a number of ways:

- The research program will require substantial, long-term funding that is sustained across administrations and political constituencies.

- The program will require intellectual leadership that extends over a substantial period of time and that is insulated from political influence.

- The program will be sustainable only if procedures for synthesizing knowledge across the various individual research activities are planned in advance.

- The program will require a cadre of investigators who are well trained for the research work.

- Research solicitations must be thoughtful, scholarly, and responsive to the intellectual resources available within the research community.

- The rigor and quality of the research review must be increased, a process that will require training reviewers and maintaining a systematic review system.

The program of research and development that we outline would require funding resources beyond those currently available to the Department of Education. The current expenditures on education research and development (R&D) are only 0.3 percent of the total national expenditures for K–12 education, a percentage far less than that devoted to R&D in other fields, such as health. The RRSG believes that the investment in education R&D should be gradually expanded to 2 to 3 percent of the total expenditures for K–12 education, a figure comparable to that in other fields. The additional R&D dollars would enormously enhance the value of the funds that are already being expended on school improvement, special education, bilingual education, professional development, and curriculum development. As such, the additional dollars spent on R&D will represent a productive investment in the education of the nation's schoolchildren.

ACKNOWLEDGMENTS

The RAND Reading Study Group and its members are most grateful to the many groups and individuals who played a role in shaping this report. First, the RRSG is indebted to the independent peer reviewers who critiqued our initial draft: Douglas Buehl, reading specialist, Madison East High School, Madison Metropolitan School District, Wisconsin; Susan Goldman, Vanderbilt University; Carol D. Lee, Northwestern University; Peter Mosenthal, Syracuse University; Charles A. Perfetti, University of Pittsburgh; Sheila A. Potter, coordinator, English Language Arts Program, Michigan Department of Education; Michael Pressley, Notre Dame University; and Robert Rueda, University of Southern California. The RRSG is also indebted to several individuals who wrote background papers: P. David Pearson, University of California, Berkeley; Diana Nicole Hamm, Michigan State University; and Jay Lemke, City University of New York.

Next, the RRSG thanks the various professional associations and the persons within them who, by individual or group response, provided valuable commentary on the RRSG's initial draft that was posted on the Achievement for All website and presented at numerous conference gatherings: the American Educational Research Association; the Center for the Improvement of Early Reading Achievement, University of Michigan; the International Reading Association; the National Association for Bilingual Education; the National Council for Teachers of English; the National Reading Conference; the Society for the Scientific Study of Reading; the Society for Text and Discourse; the University of Michigan School of Education graduate students and faculty; and the Washington Area Reading Group. Individual practitioners and scholars, too numerous to list by name, independently sent us constructive comments and suggestions on the draft report; we thank each and every one of them for taking the time to thoughtfully review the RRSG's initial draft.

The study group wishes to acknowledge several other persons who were connected with the development of this document and who provided guidance throughout the process: Thomas Glennan, Jr., and P. Michael Timpane, senior advisors for education policy at RAND, and Fredric Mosher, RAND consultant. This product benefited from the attention of Gina Schuyler, project coordinator, and Rita Foy Moss, U.S. Department of Education, who assisted in staffing the RRSG. The RRSG also recognizes JoAn Chun and Jennifer Cromley, who contributed their efforts in the latter stage of product development. Finally, the study group extends its special appreciation to Anne P. Sweet, senior researcher on reading literacy, U.S. Department of Education, who served as lead staff on this project while in residence at RAND. She provided invaluable management and support to the study group's work as it proceeded from start to finish.

Catherine Snow, *Chair*
RAND Reading Study Group

RAND READING STUDY GROUP AND RAND STAFF

RAND READING STUDY GROUP MEMBERS

Catherine Snow, Harvard University, *RRSG Chair*

Donna Alvermann, University of Georgia

Janice Dole, University of Utah

Jack Fletcher, University of Texas at Houston

Georgia Earnest García, University of Illinois at Urbana-Champaign

Irene Gaskins, The Benchmark School

Arthur Graesser, University of Memphis

John T. Guthrie, University of Maryland

Michael L. Kamil, Stanford University

William Nagy, Seattle Pacific University

Annemarie Sullivan Palincsar, University of Michigan

Dorothy Strickland, Rutgers University

Frank Vellutino, State University of New York at Albany

Joanna Williams, Columbia University

CONTRIBUTING RAND STAFF

Thomas Glennan, Jr., senior advisor for education policy

Fredric Mosher, RAND consultant

Gina Schuyler, project coordinator

Anne P. Sweet, senior researcher on reading literacy, *Lead RRSG Staff*

P. Michael Timpane, senior advisor for education policy

Chapter One

INTRODUCTION

This report presents a proposed reading research agenda drafted by the RAND Reading Study Group (RRSG). It addresses issues that the community of reading researchers urgently needs to address over the next 10 to 15 years. As a basis for the proposed agenda, this report maps the fields of knowledge that are relevant to the goal of improving reading outcomes and identifies some key areas in which research would help the education community reach that goal. The major challenges in the area of reading education include understanding how children learn to comprehend the material they are reading, how to design and deliver instruction that promotes comprehension, how to assess comprehension, and how to prevent poor comprehension outcomes. This report outlines a research agenda that will help the education profession meet these challenges.

STUDY METHODOLOGY

RAND and the RRSG engaged a wide range of people in the development of this report. This level of input was intended to both expand the study group's thinking and contribute to the development of informed research and practice communities. The initial draft of this report was released in February 2001 and was widely distributed. The draft was also published on RAND's public Achievement for All website (www.rand.org/multi/achievementforall) along with external reviews from eight experts in reading research and practice. The website encouraged visitors to comment directly on the draft report and to participate in discussions about key issues related to reading. In addition, the draft report was the subject of discussion at many professional meetings. The RRSG used the public critiques to guide the *Plan for Revision*, a second version of the draft report, which was posted on the Achievement for All website in April 2001.

This report incorporates both the ideas offered in the *Plan for Revision* and additional deliberation by the RRSG. It is intended to provide a baseline for future documents that the education field should regularly produce and revise over the course of a long-term program of research and development (R&D) for improved reading comprehension. This report addresses the issue of promoting proficient reading, while focusing on the development of reading comprehension and the capacity to acquire knowledge through reading.

Various models of reading comprehension are supported by empirical evidence. However, the sizable gaps in the knowledge base make it difficult to choose among the models or to see how the models fit together to form a larger picture of proficient reading. Some of these gaps, furthermore, have real consequences for the capacity of the education community to improve reading outcomes. Thus, although research has provided some amount of knowledge about the domain of comprehension, it has been insufficient in providing a basis to redesign comprehension instruction. Addressing the gaps in the knowledge base will require, among other things, developing networks of communication among researchers currently working in several different research traditions relevant to comprehension. Closing the knowledge gap will also require working with teachers and teacher educators to build rigorous knowledge bases for both research and practice that are mutually accessible and usable.

RESEARCH CHALLENGES

What is the core challenge facing those in the field of research on proficient reading? It is the widely held belief that proficient reading is the natural, and perhaps inevitable, outcome when good reading instruction is available through grade 3. The core challenge is to help researchers, practitioners, and policymakers understand that marshaling the forces of both reading researchers and educators to ensure that all children are reading at the third-grade level by grade 3 is only the first step in promoting proficient reading. Some of those good third-grade readers will progress on their own to proficiency in reading, but many will not. Many will need explicit, well-designed instruction in reading comprehension to continue making progress. Yet, we[1] do not have an adequate research base for designing and implementing effective reading comprehension instruction.

A core problem for researchers interested in the issue of reading comprehension is the absence of an adequately rich set of theories and models to provide a coherent foundation for their work. This set of theories needs to be sufficiently complex to encompass the array of factors involved in proficient reading; simultaneously, it needs to be informed by the multiple perspectives (including educational, cognitive, linguistic, sociolinguistic, discourse analytic, and cultural perspectives) that have been brought to bear in the design and conduct of literacy research. Considerable research has been directed at issues of reading

---

[1]The first-person plural when used in this report refers to the RRSG as a group.

comprehension, but those research efforts have been neither systematic nor interconnected.

Thus, when a sixth-grade teacher turns to published research with the question "What should I do with my students who don't understand their history texts or can't learn from reading science texts?" no consensus answer is available. Teachers with such questions encounter only a partial knowledge base, and one that does not sufficiently acknowledge the exigencies of the classroom.

Research-based knowledge about comprehension does not simultaneously attend to the demands of reading to learn during content-area instruction while still learning to read, and it does not incorporate responses to the reading profiles of many of the students in today's classrooms. Given the enormous educational importance of promoting both reading comprehension and learning among elementary and secondary students, it is crucial to organize what we know about these topics, define what we need to know, and pursue the research that will be most important for improving teacher preparation, classroom instruction, and student achievement.

The goal the RRSG set for itself, then, was to summarize the state of research and research-based practice in the field of reading comprehension as a prerequisite to generating a well-founded agenda for future research that will inform practice in this area. The proposed research agenda builds on a number of recent efforts to summarize the knowledge base in the field of reading. These efforts include the National Research Council report *Preventing Reading Difficulties in Young Children* (Snow, Burns, & Griffin, Eds., 1998); the report of the National Reading Panel, *Teaching Children to Read: An Evidence-Based Assessment of the Scientific Research Literature on Reading and Its Implications for Reading Instruction* (NRP, 2000); and the recently published edition of the *Handbook of Reading Research* (Kamil, Mosenthal, Pearson, & Barr, Eds., 2000). Given the availability of these and other older sources, the RRSG did not attempt an exhaustive synthesis of the knowledge base concerning reading and its implications for instruction and assessment of the general population; in many cases, the RRSG provides examples to support its claims instead of documenting them comprehensively. Thus, the research agenda presented in this document should be seen as a stimulus to ongoing discussion rather than a summative statement.

The program of reading research that the RRSG is proposing fits into the larger context of research on reading in the United States. Robust efforts funded in large part through the National Institute of Child Health and Human Development (NICHD) originally focused on beginning reading instruction but are now being expanded to include the literacy development of preschool-aged, adolescent, and adult literacy learners. The Office of Bilingual Education and

Minority Languages Affairs funded an initial study on bilingual readers, and NICHD together with the Department of Education's Office of Educational Research and Improvement (OERI) subsequently launched a substantial effort focused on analyzing the transfer from reading in Spanish to reading in English. Future funding will not be limited to Spanish-English bilingual readers. The Interagency Education Research Initiative (IERI)—funded jointly by the National Science Foundation, OERI, and NICHD—is funding efforts that bring early research to scale with some emphasis on the use of technology. Thus, the reading research program we propose seeks to fill gaps left by the existing research efforts, while being cohesively organized around a central set of issues facing practitioners.

The remainder of this chapter presents the RRSG's motivation for its focus on reading comprehension and Chapter Two presents our formal definition of reading comprehension. Chapter Three examines the variability in each element of reading comprehension incorporated in our definition; the brief overviews of research included in Chapter Three are supplemented by Appendix A, in which the research base in each domain of reading comprehension is more systematically reviewed. In Chapter Four, we justify and discuss the three critical components of a long-term research agenda for improving reading comprehension: classroom instruction, teacher preparation and professional development, and appropriate assessment. Finally, in Chapter Five, we discuss some strategies, criteria, and prerequisites for the successful pursuit of this agenda.

THE ISSUES MOTIVATING THIS STUDY

The proposed research agenda is built on a number of overarching issues of concern to the research and practice communities.

The demand for literacy skills is high and getting higher. The U.S. economy today demands a universally higher level of literacy achievement than at any other time in history, and it is reasonable to believe that the demand for a literate populace will increase in the future. An employment market with few blue-collar jobs but many service-related and information-based jobs is increasingly demanding high school graduation as the minimum educational credential for employment. Moreover, advanced vocational or academic training is a requirement now for a wide variety of positions that previously might have gone to high school dropouts. Thus, ensuring advanced literacy achievement for all students is no longer a luxury but an economic necessity. Using computers and accessing the Internet make large demands on individuals' literacy skills; in some cases, this new technology requires readers to have novel literacy skills, and little is known about how to analyze or teach those skills.

The level of reading skills remains stagnant. Reading scores of high school students, as reported by the National Assessment of Educational Progress (NAEP), have not improved over the last 30 years. Although mathematics scores have improved, reading scores stubbornly remain flat. In fact, the reading achievement of grade 12 students has recently decreased significantly. With few exceptions, indicators of achievement in states and school districts have shown no or only slow growth across grades in the past ten years.

Further, in international comparisons of performance on reading assessments, U.S. 11th graders have placed very close to the bottom, behind students from the Philippines, Indonesia, Brazil, and other developing nations. This poor performance contrasts with rankings in grade 4, when U.S. students have placed close to the top in international comparisons. These findings confirm teachers' impressions that many students who read well enough in the primary grades confront difficulties with reading thereafter.[2]

Reading comprehension instruction is often minimal or ineffective. Teachers often assume that students will learn to comprehend merely by reading. Although some will, many others will not. Teaching children to comprehend is challenging because reading is complex. Students who are good comprehenders use strategies in reading to learn new concepts, get deeply involved in what they are reading, critically evaluate what they read, and apply their new knowledge to solve practical as well as intellectual problems. But many students fail at doing these things. One problem is that classroom materials are often so difficult to comprehend or uninteresting that many students cannot or will not read them. Moreover, comprehension instruction tends to be emphasized less in subject-matter classrooms where teachers are focused on content. Sometimes children miss early opportunities to learn because comprehension instruction is delayed until the later elementary grades, even though a focus on comprehension is desirable from the very beginning of reading instruction. In the absence of a consensus on standards for comprehension achievement and instruction throughout the elementary, middle, and secondary grades, it would not be surprising if a child's access to excellent reading comprehension instruction were not systematic or sustained.

Reading instruction is seldom effectively integrated with content-area instruction. Children need to read well if they are to learn what is expected of them in school beyond grade 3. Teaching in the content areas relies on texts as a major

---

[2]The fall in rankings from grade 4 to grade 11 may reflect the fact that more U.S. students continue their education, so more students were included in the secondary education scores than were included in the primary school scores. However, the current insistence on "educating all students" implies that we cannot hide behind selection bias as an excuse for the poor performance of high school students.

source of instructional content. These texts are not designed as a context for comprehension instruction, but comprehension instruction that uses these texts may be crucial if students are to understand or learn from them. Content-area teachers presuppose adequate literacy skills among their students and they are typically not well prepared to teach students with below-average literacy skills, despite the aspiration voiced by noted educator Sterl Artley: "every teacher a teacher of reading." At the same time, specific reading comprehension tasks must be mastered in the context of specific subject matter. Learning discipline-specific vocabulary words, text structures, methods, and perspectives involves acquiring both content knowledge and reading skills simultaneously. The relatively poor performance of U.S. middle school and secondary school students in comparisons of international science and reading scores likely reflects in part their poor performance as readers.

The achievement gap between children of different demographic groups persists. Attention to reading comprehension is crucial in a society determined to minimize the achievement gaps between European-American children and those from groups historically ill served in U.S. schools, between suburban and urban or rural children, and between middle-class and working-class children. NAEP scores, for example, show that 17-year-old African-American students score at the level of 13-year-old European-American students—a gap that has decreased only minimally in the past 20 years. This large and persistent gap in reading achievement in the later elementary and secondary grades relates to differences in achievement in other content areas and to differences in high-school dropout and college entrance rates.

The explanations for these differences in reading achievement vary. Some portion of the gap may be explained by cultural and social issues, reflected in the increasing difficulty of making school-based literacy relevant to learners from some groups. For example, different readers interpret the reading task differently in ways that are socially and culturally influenced, or are confronted with school-based definitions of literacy that are not congruent with those learned at home or in their local communities. A large portion of the gap in reading achievement can be related to the greater likelihood that Latino and African-American students are growing up in poverty and attending schools with fewer resources, fewer experienced teachers, and that have less of a focus on academics. Members of some ethnic and racial groups, even if they are middle class, are less likely to have access to excellent instruction than are European-American children; they are also likely to face lower performance expectations from teachers and school administrators.

Second-language students face particular challenges in the later grades when they are pushed beyond the simple second- and third-grade English texts. The texts they encounter in the later grades often incorporate sophisticated vocabulary and complex linguistic and discourse structures that second-language speakers have not yet mastered. In addition, the greater amount of cognitive effort required when reading in a second language may discourage second-language learners from engaging in the reading practice they need to become more proficient. From a sociocultural perspective, both the process (the way in which the instruction is delivered and the social interactions that contextualize the learning experience) and the content (the focus of instruction) are of major importance in helping explain group differences in outcome.

High-stakes tests are affecting reading comprehension instruction in unknown ways. The standards-based movement in education is an effort to improve schooling for all children by establishing clear achievement standards. Children are tested to provide information to parents, teachers, and schools about the degree of compliance with the standards. Increasingly, the failure to meet the standards is being associated with child-specific sanctions, such as retaining the child in grade or withholding a high school diploma. The achievement tests to which these high stakes are attached often reflect reading comprehension ability, even when the specific goal of the test is to assess knowledge in the content areas. The data available to date about the effect of high-stakes tests on student achievement are insufficient and conflicting. No research has addressed how poor comprehenders are selectively affected either by the tests themselves or by the various consequences associated with them.

The preparation of teachers does not adequately address children's needs for reading comprehension instruction. Research has shown that child outcomes are related to the quality of the instruction they receive, which in turn reflects teacher preparation and ongoing teacher professional development. Yet teacher preparation and professional development programs are inadequate in the crucial domain of reading comprehension, in part because the solid, systematic research base that should provide a foundation for teacher preparation does not exist.

Making good on the federal investment in education requires more knowledge about reading comprehension. Recent federal legislation focused on literacy has had as a major goal the introduction of instructional practices that are based on well-founded research. Efforts funded through the Reading Excellence Act (REA), for example, are focused on beginning reading instruction. However, a child who successfully develops beginning reading skills may not automatically become a skilled reader. Large numbers of children who have successfully acquired beginning reading skills later fall behind in their ability to deal with school reading tasks—a phenomenon that experienced teachers call the "fourth grade slump." Explicit instruction in reading comprehension is essential for many children to ensure their transition from beginning reading to reading proficiently. Presently, the research base necessary to inform teachers and schools about best practices for teaching reading in the post-primary grades is not adequately developed. The recent federal investment through the REA and its successor programs, Reading First and Early Reading First (totaling more than $5 billion over the next five years), will be lost unless the knowledge base on reading comprehension is further developed.

MUCH IS ALREADY KNOWN ABOUT IMPROVING COMPREHENSION

Given the overarching issues presented in this chapter, the task of developing a research agenda that will contribute to improved reading instruction may seem formidable. Nonetheless, we are encouraged by the fact that much is already known about addressing the practical challenges of improving reading comprehension outcomes.

First, research has provided some of the prerequisites to successful reading comprehension. For example, reading comprehension capacity builds on successful initial reading instruction and the fact that children who can read words accurately and rapidly have a good foundation for progressing well in comprehension. We know that children with good oral language skills (large oral vocabularies and good listening comprehension) and with well-developed stores of world knowledge are likely to become good comprehenders. We know that social interaction in homes and classrooms, as well as in communities and in the larger sociocultural context, enhances students' motivation and their participation in literate communities and helps form students' identities as readers, thus increasing their access to written text. We know that children who have had a rich exposure to literacy experiences are more likely to succeed. We know about several instructional practices that are related to good reading outcomes, although such knowledge is much more extensive for initial reading than it is for later reading. Finally, we know that instruction based on an appropriate and well-articulated alignment between curriculum and assessment can improve performance in reading as well as in other areas.

We also know about several approaches to education and to reading instruction that do not work. We know, for example, that many approaches to compensatory education for socially, economically, and educationally disadvantaged groups do not promote success in reading comprehension. We know as well that identifying children as learning disabled, without offering specific instructional treatments tailored to their individual needs, fails to generate reading comprehension gains. We know that current approaches to teaching second-language learners, whether in English as a Second Language (ESL), bilingual, or all-English settings, often do not address the particular challenges of reading comprehension.

We know that teaching is so complex that the current teacher education programs cannot adequately prepare novice teachers to engage in practice that reflects the existing knowledge base about reading. We know that this situation is particularly critical for special education, ESL, and bilingual teachers. Although these teachers require an even deeper understanding of reading, language, curricula, and instructional practices than do mainstream teachers, in fact they have even fewer opportunities in their preparation programs to acquire this expertise. We know that pre-service preparation and professional development in the domain of early reading instruction are improving and are increasingly incorporating information from research about the characteristics of good instruction. However, such is not the case for reading comprehension instruction in the later elementary grades.

We know that retention in grade (an increasingly frequent consequence of failure on high-stakes assessments) does not improve long-term reading achievement without specialized instruction. Finally, although we have a fairly long list of instructional strategies that have been shown to be effective in targeted interventions or experimental settings, we need to know how to implement these teaching approaches on a large-scale basis in a coherent reading program that spans the elementary, middle, and high school grades.

THE NEED FOR A DEFINITION OF READING COMPREHENSION

The larger agenda that concerns the RRSG is the promotion of proficient reading. The RRSG sees achieving reading proficiency as a long-term developmental process; what constitutes "reading well" is different at different points in the reader's development. The end point—proficient adult reading—encompasses the capacity to read, with ease and interest, a wide variety of different kinds of materials for varying purposes and to read with comprehension even when the material is neither easy to understand nor intrinsically interesting. Adult reading involves reading for pleasure, learning, and analysis, and it represents a prerequisite to many forms of employment, to informed participation in the democratic process, to optimal participation in the education of one's children, and to gaining access to cultural capital.

A formal definition of reading comprehension may seem unnecessary because the term is used so widely and its meaning is assumed to be generally understood. Teachers think of reading comprehension as what students are taught to do in reading instruction during the early school years and as the reading capacities they are expected to display throughout the middle and high school years.[3] Taxpayers and employers think of reading comprehension as one of the capabilities that high school graduates should have acquired during their years in school. University faculty view high levels of reading comprehension as a prerequisite to a student's success. Yet, coming to a formal definition that is widely accepted turns out to be rather difficult. We believe that it is necessary, as a prerequisite to mapping the domains of knowledge relevant to formulating a research agenda in this area, to define comprehension in a way that clearly specifies its key elements. In the next chapter, we present such a definition, which we elaborate on in Chapter Three by describing variability within the elements of the definition.

---

[3]Reading comprehension is usually a primary focus of instruction in the post-primary grades, after readers have largely mastered word recognition skills, although comprehension of text should be an integral part of reading instruction with beginning readers as well. Instruction in oral language, vocabulary, and listening comprehension should be a focus starting in preschool and continuing throughout the elementary grades.

Chapter Two

DEFINING COMPREHENSION

We define reading comprehension as the process of simultaneously extracting and constructing meaning through interaction and involvement with written language. We use the words *extracting* and *constructing* to emphasize both the importance and the insufficiency of the text as a determinant of reading comprehension. Comprehension entails three elements:[1]

- The *reader* who is doing the comprehending

- The *text* that is to be comprehended

- The *activity* in which comprehension is a part.

In considering the reader, we include all the capacities, abilities, knowledge, and experiences that a person brings to the act of reading. Text is broadly construed to include any printed text or electronic text. In considering activity, we include the purposes, processes, and consequences associated with the act of reading.

These three dimensions define a phenomenon that occurs within a larger *sociocultural context* (see Figure 1) that shapes and is shaped by the reader and that interacts with each of the three elements. The identities and capacities of

---

[1]It should be noted that we are using terms that others have also used in defining reading comprehension, sometimes in similar and sometimes in slightly different ways. Galda and Beach (2001), for example, define context in a way that is not dissimilar from ours, whereas Spiro and Myers (1984) use context in a way that emphasizes culture less and task or purpose more. Many authors identify much the same list of attributes (purpose, interest, text, knowledge, strategy use, etc.) as we do, but Blachowicz and Ogle (2001), for example, distribute these attributes over the categories of individual and social processes rather than group them as we do. Pearson (2001) and Alexander and Jetton (2000) identify reader (learner), text, and context as key dimensions, without including activity as a separate dimension at the same level of analysis. The National Reading Panel report focuses on text and reader as sources of variability (NRP, 2000). Gaskins, in analyses with a variety of colleagues (e.g., Gaskins, 1998; Gaskins et al., 1993; Gaskins & Elliot, 1991), has identified comprehension as requiring the reader to take charge of text, task, and context variables, presumably an implicit acknowledgment that text, task, and context are all important in defining reading comprehension and can be obstacles to comprehension, while at the same time the reader is seen as the most central element.

readers, the texts that are available and valued, and the activities in which readers are engaged with those texts are all influenced by, and in some cases determined by, the sociocultural context. The sociocultural context mediates students' experiences, just as students' experiences influence the context. We elaborate on each element in subsequent sections.

Reader, text, and activity are also interrelated in dynamic ways that vary across pre-reading, reading, and post-reading. We consider each of these three "microperiods" in reading because it is important to distinguish between what the reader brings to reading and what the reader takes from reading. Each act of reading is potentially a microdevelopmental process. For example, in the pre-reading microperiod, the reader arrives with a host of characteristics, including cognitive, motivational, language, and non-linguistic capabilities, along with a particular level of fluency. During the reading microperiod, some of these reader characteristics may change. Likewise, during the post-reading micro-period of the same reading event, some of these same reader characteristics, or

RAND*MR1465-1*

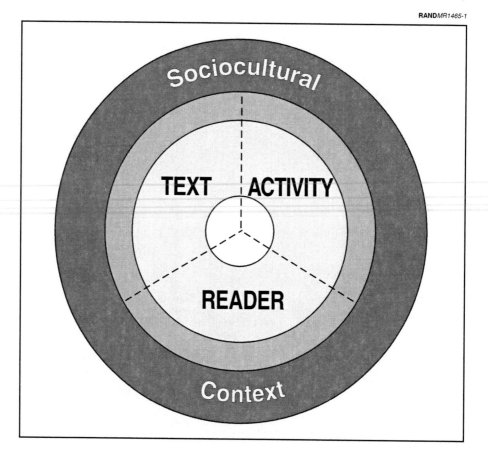

Figure 2.1—A Heuristic for Thinking About Reading Comprehension

other reader characteristics, may change again. Much research related to reading comprehension has focused on specific factors (e.g., vocabulary knowledge) without specifying either that the effect of that factor reflects a relationship among reader, text, and activity or that the factor may change from pre-reading to reading to post-reading.

The process of comprehension also has a macrodevelopmental aspect. It changes over time, as the reader matures and develops cognitively, as the reader gains increasing experience with more challenging texts, and as the reader benefits from instruction. From among the many factors influencing the macrodevelopment of comprehension, we have selected instruction, particularly classroom instruction, for special attention as we sketch the research agenda needed to improve comprehension outcomes.

THE READER

To comprehend, a reader must have a wide range of capacities and abilities. These include cognitive capacities (e.g., attention, memory, critical analytic ability, inferencing, visualization ability), motivation (a purpose for reading, an interest in the content being read, self-efficacy as a reader), and various types of knowledge (vocabulary, domain and topic knowledge, linguistic and discourse knowledge, knowledge of specific comprehension strategies). Of course, the specific cognitive, motivational, and linguistic capacities and the knowledge base called on in any act of reading comprehension depend on the texts in use and the specific activity in which one is engaged.

Fluency can be conceptualized as both an antecedent to and a consequence of comprehension. Some aspects of fluent, expressive reading may depend on a thorough understanding of a text. However, some components of fluency—quick and efficient recognition of words and at least some aspects of syntactic parsing—appear to be prerequisites for comprehension.

As a reader begins to read and completes whatever activity is at hand, some of the knowledge and capabilities of the reader change. For example, a reader might increase domain knowledge during reading. Similarly, vocabulary, linguistic, or discourse knowledge might increase. Fluency could also increase as a function of the additional practice in reading. Motivational factors, such as self-concept or interest in the topic, might change in either a positive or a negative direction during a successful or an unsuccessful reading experience.

Another important source of changes in knowledge and capacities is the instruction that a reader receives. Appropriate instruction will foster reading comprehension, which is defined in two ways—the comprehension of the text under current consideration and comprehension capacities more generally.

Thus, although teachers may focus their content area instruction on helping students understand the material, an important concurrent goal is helping students learn how to become self-regulated, active readers who have a variety of strategies to help them comprehend. Effective teachers incorporate both goals into their comprehension instruction. They have a clear understanding of which students need which type of instruction for which texts, and they give students the instruction they need to meet both short-term and long-term comprehension goals.

THE TEXT

The features of text have a large effect on comprehension. Comprehension does not occur by simply extracting meaning from text. During reading, the reader constructs different representations of the text that are important for comprehension. These representations include, for example, the surface code (the exact wording of the text), the text base (idea units representing the meaning), and a representation of the mental models embedded in the text. The proliferation of computers and electronic text has led us to broaden the definition of text to include electronic text and multimedia documents in addition to conventional print. Electronic text can present particular challenges to comprehension, such as dealing with the non-linear nature of hypertext, but it also offers the potential for supporting the comprehension of complex texts, for example, through hyperlinks to definitions or translations of difficult words or to paraphrasing of complex sentences.

Texts can be difficult or easy, depending on factors inherent in the text, on the relationship between the text and the knowledge and abilities of the reader, and on the activities in which the reader is engaged. For example, the content presented in the text has a critical bearing on reading comprehension. A reader's domain knowledge interacts with the content of the text in comprehension. In addition to content, the vocabulary load of the text and its linguistic structure, discourse style, and genre also interact with the reader's knowledge. When too many of these factors are not matched to a reader's knowledge and experience, the text may be too difficult for optimal comprehension to occur. Further, various activities are better suited to some texts than to others. For example, electronic texts that are the product of Internet searches typically need to be scanned for relevance and for reliability, unlike assigned texts that are meant to be studied more deeply. Electronic texts that incorporate hyperlinks and hypermedia introduce some complications in defining comprehension because they require skills and abilities beyond those required for the comprehension of conventional, linear print.

The challenge of teaching reading comprehension is heightened in the current educational era because all students are expected to read more text and more complex texts. Schools can no longer track students so that only those with highly developed reading skills take the more reading-intensive courses. All students now need to read high-level texts with comprehension to pass high-stakes exams and to make themselves employable.

THE ACTIVITY

Reading does not occur in a vacuum. It is done for a purpose, to achieve some end. Activity refers to this dimension of reading. A reading activity involves one or more purposes, some operations to process the text at hand, and the consequences of performing the activity. Prior to reading, a reader has a purpose, which can be either externally imposed (e.g., completing a class assignment) or internally generated (wanting to program a VCR). The purpose is influenced by a cluster of motivational variables, including interest and prior knowledge. The initial purposes can change as the reader reads. That is, a reader might encounter information that raises new questions that make the original purpose either incomplete or irrelevant. When the purpose is externally mandated, as in instruction, the reader might accept the purpose and complete the activity; for example, if the assignment is "read a paragraph in order to write a summary," the compliant student will accept that purpose and engage in reading operations designed to address it. If the reader does not fully accept the mandated purpose, internally generated purposes may conflict with the externally mandated purpose. Such conflicts may lead to incomplete comprehension. For example, if students fail to see the relevance of an assignment, they may not read purposively, thus compromising their comprehension of the text.

During reading, the reader processes the text with regard to the purpose. Processing the text involves, beyond decoding, higher-level linguistic and semantic processing and monitoring. Each process is more or less important in different types of reading, including skimming (getting only the gist of text) and studying (reading text with the intent of retaining the information for a period of time).

Finally, the consequences of reading are part of the activity. Some reading activities lead to an increase in the *knowledge* a reader has. For example, reading the historical novel *Andersonville* may increase the reader's knowledge about the U.S. Civil War, even though the reader's initial purpose may have been enjoyment. The American history major who reads an assigned text about the Civil War may experience similar consequences, although the reading activity was undertaken for the explicit purpose of learning. Another consequence of reading activities is finding out how to do something. These *application* consequences are often related to the goal of the reader. Repairing a bicycle or preparing bouillabaisse from a recipe are examples of applications. As with knowledge consequences, application consequences may or may not be related to the original purposes. Finally, other reading activities have *engagement* as their consequences. Reading the latest Tom Clancy novel might keep the reader involved while on vacation at the beach. We are not suggesting, however, that engagement occurs only with fiction. Good comprehenders can be engaged in many different types of text.

Knowledge, application, and engagement can be viewed as direct consequences of the reading activity. Activities may also have other, longer-term consequences. Any knowledge (or application) acquired during reading for enjoyment also becomes part of the knowledge that a reader brings to the next reading experience. Learning new vocabulary, acquiring incidental knowledge about Civil War battles or bouillabaisse ingredients, or discovering a new interest might all be consequences of reading with comprehension.

THE CONTEXT

One important set of reading activities occurs in the context of instruction. Understanding how the reader's purpose for reading and operations are shaped by instruction, and how short- and long-term consequences are influenced by instruction, constitutes a major issue within the research agenda we propose.

When we think about the context of learning to read, we think mostly of classrooms. Of course, children bring to their classrooms vastly varying capacities and understandings about reading, which are in turn influenced, or in some cases determined, by their experiences in their homes and neighborhoods. Further, classrooms and schools themselves reflect the neighborhood context and the economic disparities of the larger society. The differences in instruction and in the availability of texts, computers, and other instructional resources between schools serving low-income neighborhoods and those serving middle-income neighborhoods are well documented.

Sociocultural and sociohistorical theories of learning and literacy describe how children acquire literacy through social interactions with more expert peers and adults. According to Vygotsky (1978), with the guidance and support of an expert, children are able to perform tasks that are slightly beyond their own independent knowledge and capability. As they become more knowledgeable and experienced with the task, the support is withdrawn, and the children internalize the new knowledge and experiences they have acquired, which results in learning. From a sociocultural perspective, both the process (the ways the instruction is delivered and the social interactions that contextualize the learning experience) and the content (the focus of instruction) are of major importance.

Tharp and Gallimore (1988) explain that children's acquisition of knowledge (and literacy) is influenced by five characteristics of the sociocultural context, which they call activity settings: the identity of the participants, how the activity is defined or executed, the timing of the activity, where it occurs, and why children should participate in the activity, or the motivation for the activity. Clearly, all five characteristics are likely to vary as a function of both economic and cultural factors.

The effects of contextual factors, including economic resources, class membership, ethnicity, neighborhood, and school culture, can be seen in oral language practices, in students' self-concepts, in the types of literacy activities in which individuals engage, in instructional history, and, of course, in the likelihood of successful outcomes. The classroom-learning environment (such as organizational grouping, inclusion of technology, or availability of materials) is an important aspect of the context that can affect the development of comprehension abilities.

Chapter Three

VARIABILITY IN READING COMPREHENSION

In this chapter, we elaborate on our definition of reading comprehension by giving examples of variations in the three reading comprehension elements—reader, text, and activity—and variations in the context in which they occur. Of course, none of these elements operates independently of the others in any authentic act of comprehension. However, we consider each in turn because each has an internal structure that deserves further consideration and that may clarify how we conceptualize these elements of reading comprehension and the interface among them.

It is somewhat difficult to treat context in the same way as reader, text, and activity because context does not simply coexist with the other elements; rather, it interacts with all of them in any part of the reading process. The selection of texts to read, notions about the appropriate purposes for or consequences of the reading activity, and many of the factors that impinge on and differentiate readers are sociocultural in nature; they vary as a function of economic resources, the local community, cultural membership, and family choice. Schools represent particular kinds of sociocultural contexts, which vary greatly for some learners and minimally for others from the contexts of home and community. We can also view classrooms as contexts with their own rules about who should be reading what text and for what purpose. These rules may be implicit or explicit, and they may be formulated to ensure that all children perform at a high level or to pose continued challenges to some children.

Each of the following sections (which deal with reader, text, activity, and context) gives an overview of what we know about variability in each domain. An extended and annotated review of what we know about variability in each element can be found in Appendix A.

VARIABILITY IN READERS

Proficient readers bring to the task of reading an array of capabilities and dispositions. Reader differences in such capabilities as fluency in word recognition, oral language ability, and domain knowledge, along with differences in such dispositions as the reader's motivation, goals, and purposes, are important sources of variability in reading comprehension. Such variables interact with one another and with the text to which the reader is exposed (the text can be narrative, expository, etc.) as determinants of performance on a given reading task (acquiring knowledge in a domain, performing a comparative analysis, solving a problem, etc.).

The capabilities and dispositions the reader brings to the task of reading, his or her engagement in and responses to given texts, and the quality of the outcomes produced by the act of reading for some purpose are, themselves, shaped by cultural and subcultural influences, socioeconomic status, home and family background, peer influences, classroom culture, and instructional history. These multiple and interacting factors influence both the inter- and intra-individual differences in reading proficiency that we must consider in defining reading comprehension as a field of study. We summarize in this chapter what we know about the dimensions of reader differences or, perhaps more precisely, what we know about the sources of variation in the functioning of the various comprehension processes in service of the various outcomes related to the act of reading for some purpose.

Sociocultural Influences

Reader variability is, to some extent, a product of the fact that children come from and learn to read in varying sociocultural contexts. We view learning and literacy as cultural and historical activities, not just because they are acquired through social interactions, but also because they represent how a specific cultural group or discourse community interprets the world and transmits this information. According to Gee (1990), an awareness of how members of particular discourse communities construct their identities as readers (through their ways of behaving, interacting, valuing, thinking, believing, speaking, reading, and writing) is one important step in understanding variability in readers. "Reading the world" (Freire, 1970), or ideology, also is an inherent characteristic of discourse. As adults, we belong to multiple discourse communities. However, the first discourse community into which children are socialized is their home and the surrounding community.

When discourse communities differ in how they view the world and differ in what social practices guide their children's instruction, conflicts are bound to occur. Schooling in the United States tends to reflect a European-American, middle-class, economically privileged view of what counts as the process and content of learning and literacy (Hernandez, 1989). All students have to learn how to adapt to school norms and mores (e.g., raise your hand to be called on, ask permission to go to the bathroom); students who are not European-American and middle class may have even more new norms and mores to learn because they typically do not belong to their teachers' primary discourse community (Cazden, 1988).

A sociocultural perspective is often invoked to help explain the poorer literacy performance of students from groups not traditionally well served in U.S. schools. In fact, though, sociocultural factors have to be considered in explaining any act of comprehension and in understanding how all students acquire reading comprehension. Understanding text in ways that satisfy U.S. teachers and the demands of U.S. test writers is an intrinsically sociocultural task. Reading research informed by a sociocultural perspective helps all parties who are interested in teaching and learning to identify and deal with the various tensions that affect the reading comprehension development, engagement, and performance of both younger and older students. Such research is crucial to designing instruction that will be effective for the full range of students in U.S. classrooms and to informing the content of preparation programs for the teachers of those students.

Group Differences

We include group differences as a focus of our interest even though they are to some extent coterminous with sociocultural and linguistic sources of variability. Indeed, a fairly large body of work has considered group membership (e.g., income-based group, racial group, ethnic group, native language group) without relating the findings to cultural factors. Further, some identified groups (e.g., children growing up in impoverished neighborhoods) or group-related factors (e.g., the smaller English vocabulary of children who speak English as a second language) cannot be defined as cultural or culture-related, and some highly influential factors (e.g., family income, attendance at good versus poor schools) are likely not only to be correlated with group membership but also to cross-cut cultural differences. For example, in research conducted with young children, Whitehurst and Lonigan (1998) reported that children from low-income homes had less experience with books, writing, rhymes, and other school-based literacy-promoting activities than did children from higher-income homes. Similarly, NAEP statistics from 1992 to the present indicate that more than 60 percent of African-American, Latino, and Native-American students scored below national normative standards for grades 4, 8, and 12.

As another example, second-language learning differentially affects literacy development depending on such factors as the age at which second-language learning is initiated, the language in which exposure to print and early literacy instruction is initiated, and the degree of support for first- and second-language learning and literacy development in both the home and school environments (Snow, Burns, & Griffin, Eds., 1998; Tabors & Snow, 2001). Thus, the relationship between reading comprehension and membership in social class and racial, ethnic, and second-language groups is a topic that merits further study. Effective instruction for ethnic and racial groups who are traditionally ill served in U.S. schools must be based on a new research effort to understand these differences in achievement, and it must be informed by newly developed assessments that better identify the capacities that children in these groups bring to the task of learning to read proficiently.

Inter-Individual Differences

Individual children vary in their reading comprehension abilities, and variability in reader characteristics may partially account for these differences. Thus, the differential development of a variety of capabilities and dispositions supporting reading comprehension may lead to patterns of relative strengths and weaknesses that are directly related to variations in reading comprehension outcomes. For example, we know from research done over the past two decades that accurate and fluent (automatic) word recognition is associated with adequate reading comprehension. We also know that language comprehension processes and higher-level processes affecting language comprehension (the application of world knowledge, reasoning, etc.) do not become fully operative in comprehending text until the child has acquired reasonable fluency (Adams, 1990; Gough & Tunmer, 1986; Hoover & Gough, 1990; Perfetti, 1985; Stanovich, 1991; Sticht & James, 1984; Vellutino et al., 1991; Vellutino, Scanlon, & Tanzman, 1994). However, we also know that fluent word recognition is not a sufficient condition for successful reading comprehension and that other variables that directly or indirectly influence language comprehension are also critically important determinants of variability in reading comprehension. These variables include (1) vocabulary and linguistic knowledge, including oral language skills and an awareness of language structures; (2) non-linguistic abilities and processes (attention, visualization, inferencing, reasoning, critical analysis, working memory, etc.); (3) engagement and motivation; (4) an understanding of the purposes and goals of reading; (5) discourse knowledge; (6) domain knowledge; and (7) cognitive and metacognitive strategy development.

Still another important determinant of variability in reading comprehension is a reader's perceptions of how competent she or he is as a reader. For both younger and older students, it is the belief in oneself (or the lack thereof) that makes a difference in how competent they feel (Pajares, 1996). Providing students who are experiencing reading difficulties with clear goals for a comprehension task and then giving them feedback on the progress they are making can lead to increased self-efficacy and a greater use of comprehension strategies (Dillon, 1989; Schunk & Rice, 1993). The degree to which these components develop in a younger or an older student may account, in part, for individual differences in the development of reading comprehension abilities.

Thus, such inter-individual differences may be usefully targeted in research evaluating the relative contributions made by individual capabilities and dispositions to variability in reading comprehension outcomes. Although these relationships between individual capacities and comprehension outcomes have been extensively studied, almost all of the work has been limited to monolingual learners; we have little idea whether the same pattern of relationships holds for second-language readers. Research that can inform better instruction in the various capacities and dispositions related to proficient reading, that can inform better assessments of these capacities and dispositions, and that can help us understand what teachers need to know about inter-individual variation across the full array of students in their classrooms is sorely needed.

Intra-Individual Differences

Students differ from one another in how diverse their reading competencies and interests are. For example, some students read stories frequently and are expert in story comprehension, whereas they rarely read electronic text and are not highly competent with computers. However, other students may be competent in reading for information on the Internet but not in interpreting linear narrative texts. Moreover, intra-individual variability in the acquisition of reading competencies can be observed during each phase of reading development, and it is sometimes manifested in the uneven development of important skills and subskills that underlie proficient reading. For example, during the beginning phases of reading development, when children are acquiring basic word-recognition, phonological-decoding (letter-sound), and text-processing skills, it is not uncommon to find a significant imbalance in the acquisition of one or another of these skills in a given child, to the detriment of that child's progress in becoming a proficient, motivated, and independent reader (Vellutino et al., 1996; Vellutino & Scanlon, in press). Similarly, the child with limited vocabulary knowledge, limited world knowledge, or both, will have difficulty comprehending texts that presuppose such knowledge, despite an adequate development of word-recognition and phonological-decoding skills.

Further, the child who does little independent reading, and who is not motivated to read extensively and diversely, may have difficulty engaging and profiting from the broad array of expository and technical texts encountered in school learning, even if he or she has no basic intellectual deficits or basic deficits in reading or oral language development. At the same time, the child who has not acquired the cognitive and metacognitive strategies and study skills necessary to use reading as an instrument of learning will undoubtedly profit less from reading in a given domain than the child who has acquired these skills, along with the disposition and tenacity to use them, even if the two children have comparable reading and oral language skills (Palincsar & Brown, 1984; Pearson & Fielding, 1991; Pressley, 2000; Tierney & Cunningham, 1984). And the child who is not motivated to acquire knowledge or to engage with the school curriculum and school learning at large risks falling behind age-mates in developing the reading comprehension capacities needed for progress in school or for employability.

Thus, patterns of strength or weakness in the domains of word-reading accuracy, fluency, comprehension strategies, vocabulary, domain knowledge, interest, and motivation can lead to performances that vary as a function of the characteristics of the text and of the task being engaged in. Little research directly addresses the issue of intra-individual differences in young and older readers. Such research could help teachers use their students' particular strengths and reading preferences to build wide-ranging reading proficiency and could inform the design of more sensitive assessments as well.

VARIABILITY IN TEXT

It has long been recognized that texts should become more complex as readers' capacities grow and that the characteristics of various genres and subject matters create varying challenges for readers. Here we consider the characteristics of text that challenge various readers, recognizing of course that ultimately it is the match or mismatch between these characteristics and a reader's capabilities that determines the likelihood of successful comprehension.

The texts that children read in today's schools are substantially more diverse than those in use several decades ago. Thirty years ago, children were assigned specific readings that were crafted for instructional purposes, or they were exposed to a select group of books in the narrative, descriptive, expository, and persuasive genres. The reading materials that made it into the "canon" did not come close to representing the array of cultures, socioeconomic classes, and perspectives of the wider society. We now live in a world that is experiencing an explosion of alternative texts that vary in content, readability levels, and genre. They incorporate multimedia and electronic options and pertain to a variety of cultures and groups. This variety makes it much more difficult for teachers to select appropriate texts for individual readers.

One place to start in understanding variability in texts is to look at all the categories of texts and the dimensions on which they vary. These categories and dimensions include the following:

- Discourse genre, such as narration, description, exposition, and persuasion.

- Discourse structure, including rhetorical composition and coherence.

- Media forms, such as textbooks, multimedia, advertisements, hypertext, and the Internet.

- Sentence difficulty, including vocabulary, syntax, and the propositional text base (the explicit meaning of the text's content drawn from propositions in the text, i.e., statements or idea units, but without more-subtle details about verb tense and deictic references [*here, there, now, then, this, that*]).

- Content, including different types of mental models, cultures, and socioeconomic strata; age-appropriate selection of subject matter; and the practices that are prominent in the culture.

- Texts with varying degrees of engagement for particular classes of readers.

The assignment of texts to specific readers becomes more difficult as alternative texts grow in number and diversity. The assignment of texts should strategically balance a student's interest in the subject matter, the student's level of development, the particular challenges faced by the student, the pedagogical goals in the curriculum, and the availability of texts. Teachers will need an enhanced knowledge of the texts that are available and access to computer technologies to help them manage the complex task of text assignment that will be expected in schools of the future.

One salient challenge is assigning texts to children at different grade levels when curricula are developed on a broad institutional scale and do not include detailed implementation instructions. We know that the assignments need to be diverse, but beyond that widespread consensus, we need an incisive plan that reflects scientific and pedagogical, rather than purely political, agendas. A large gap needs to be filled between the available electronic and multimedia materials and teachers' understanding of how the materials should be integrated with the reading curriculum. There currently is a paucity of well-written textbooks that promote understanding at a deep conceptual level, as opposed to the shallow knowledge that has pervaded our school systems. The texts selected for a child need to be sufficiently challenging and engaging in addition to being appropriate for expanding his or her comprehension proficiency. Otherwise, the child will not be intrinsically motivated to continue literacy development throughout his or her lifetime.

Contextual factors influence variability in access to texts and in the perceived difficulty and appropriateness of texts. Duke (2000) has documented that children who attend schools in poor districts have many fewer texts available than do children who attend schools in richer areas; the availability of texts in homes and libraries varies similarly. Texts that treat certain social issues or that require an interpretation and appreciation of alternative perspectives may be considered inappropriate by parents from some cultural or religious groups. Texts at an appropriate instructional level may be rejected as too babyish by older learners; paradoxically, texts that seem too difficult may be read successfully if the topic is sufficiently interesting and relevant to the learner. Text factors thus interact with reader, activity, and context in determining the difficulty of comprehension.

The importance of research on text factors to the design of effective instruction and informative assessments is obvious. A more robust research basis for preparing teachers to select and use texts optimally is also clearly needed.

VARIABILITY IN ACTIVITY

We know that many instructional activities can improve comprehension. Yet, a major and persistent issue of concern in U.S. schooling is how infrequent and ineffective the instructional activities focused on teaching comprehension are (Durkin, 1978–79). Our goal in this section is to elaborate on the definition of reading comprehension we provided in Chapter Two by identifying some dimensions along which activities included in reading comprehension instruction may vary.

We discuss instruction under the heading "activity" even though activity is a larger category than instruction. Activity refers to the acts a reader engages in with a text, and it encompasses purpose, operations, and consequences. Given the focus of this document on research to improve reading outcomes, we concentrate on the instructional contexts for reading activity. For many school-aged children, little reading activity occurs outside the classroom context; for them, instructional activities represent the only opportunity for them to read.

Variability in activity is generated by the various purposes for reading. Some purposes are self-generated, such as reading for pleasure, reading to assemble a piece of furniture, or reading to learn about dinosaurs. Other purposes may be teacher imposed: reading to answer some questions, reading to write a book report, or reading to prepare for Friday's test. When the teacher-imposed purpose is unclear to the learner, or in conflict with the learner's purpose, comprehension may well be disrupted.

One frequent teacher goal is to help students understand a particular text, either to enjoy it or to learn from it. Since the text is potentially difficult for students, teachers employ various instructional techniques that support reading. These instructional techniques target particular operations that are part of the reading activity. For example, teachers may build prerequisite background knowledge or present students with key concepts and vocabulary critical to an upcoming text (Dole et al., 1991; Graves, Cooke, & LaBerge, 1983; Langer, 1984). Content-area teachers may provide specific instructional scaffolds for their poor comprehenders who are trying to understand and learn from their difficult science and history textbooks. Another possible goal of comprehension instruction is to help students learn how to become self-regulated, active readers who use various strategies for comprehension. These comprehension strategies are procedures and routines that readers themselves apply across a number of different texts (NRP, 2000). For example, teachers may teach students to activate their own background knowledge, to draw inferences as they read, or to restate information in the text (Chan, Cole, & Barfett, 1987; Idol-Maestas, 1985; Schumaker et al., 1982). The difference between the two goals of comprehension instruction lies in the intended outcome—immediate understanding versus long-term improvement of comprehension capacity. Ideally, of course, instruction addresses both goals.

Successful comprehension can be characterized by considerable variability in a reader's reliance on the various operations involved in reading: concentrating on the task at hand, reading words, reading fluently, parsing syntactically, constructing a propositional text base, constructing mental models, generating inferences, monitoring comprehension, and using deep comprehension strategies. Each operation reflects specific reader capacities and, at the same time, is facilitated or impeded by the features of the text being read. Although some level of success at concentrating on the task of reading, reading words, and parsing sentences is a prerequisite to any success at comprehension, the degree of ease with and reliance on the other operations is evidently highly variable. Some instructional activities target specific operations, whereas successful readers evidently engage spontaneously in other activities. We know very little about the degree and sources of variation in the functioning of these operations across the full range of readers. Until we know more, we cannot help teachers to design effective instruction for students with widely varying capacities or to assess their students' instructional needs.

Of course, it is the variation in consequences that is of the greatest ultimate importance. Some classroom-structured reading activities generate important changes in the reader's capacity to comprehend an array of texts and to function as a self-regulated reader. Others, as noted above, may focus more exclusively on improving students' comprehension of the specific text under consideration. Exploring the instructional techniques that generate long-term improvements in learners' capacities to read with comprehension for the purposes of learning, applying knowledge, and being engaged is the highest priority identified for the research agenda we propose here.

VARIABILITY IN THE CONTEXT

In the previous sections on variability in the reader, text, and activity, we suggested how contextual factors ranging from economic circumstances to social group membership to classroom organization can influence reading comprehension, so we do not reiterate those differences here. We underscore the fact that contextual factors operate at many levels to influence the reader, the text, and the activity in profound ways. For example, the availability and the variability of resources matter greatly when one considers the surrounding community, the school district, the school building, and the classroom and how each varies singly and in combination as a function of context.

Perhaps the most alarming aspect of the variability in context is the degree to which the quality of instruction in reading varies between schools serving economically secure, English-speaking, European-American families and those serving economically marginalized families and families from other ethnic and linguistic groups. Not surprisingly, outcomes vary just as radically. Reading comprehension, like instruction and learning, is inextricably linked to and affected by larger sociocultural contexts. Understanding the full complexity of reading comprehension requires acknowledging that it is a cognitive, linguistic, and cultural activity.

It is possible to present a fairly extensive overview of the dimensions of variability associated primarily with the reader; our somewhat briefer discussions of variability deriving from text or from activity reflect the relative weight of available research evidence (see Appendix A). Previously articulated models of reading (Jenkins, 1976; see Alexander & Jetton, 2000; Graves & Graves, 1994; Graves, Graves, & Braaten, 1996, for discussions of the tetrahedral model) have certainly pointed to reader, task, and text as three elements of interest. Nonetheless, research has focused primarily on the reader, locating explanations for failure and targeting procedures for improvement there. We argue that creatively designing an instructional activity is just as important to improving reading comprehension as selecting appropriate texts. The role and challenge of the text expand, furthermore, as novel electronic and multimedia texts become increasingly important domains for reading.

In the next chapter, we turn to a more explicit consideration of our proposed research agenda. The overarching goal of this agenda is improving reading comprehension outcomes. The subtopics we discuss are instruction and classroom practices, teacher preparation, and assessment.

Chapter Four

A RESEARCH AGENDA FOR IMPROVING READING COMPREHENSION

In this report, the RRSG characterizes reading comprehension in a way that the group believes will help organize research and development activities in the domain of reading comprehension. In Chapter Two, we provided a working definition for reading comprehension and outlined a framework including three core elements—reader, text, and activity—which are situated in a larger sociocultural context. Chapter Three elaborated on the elements by describing what we know about variation within them. In this chapter, the RRSG proposes a research agenda that prioritizes three specific domains of reading comprehension for future research: instruction, teacher preparation, and assessment. In making these proposals, the RRSG emphasizes the need for research that builds on what is already known, that will contribute to better theories of reading development, and that will produce knowledge that is usable both in classrooms and in policymaking arenas. To that end, this chapter describes what is already known within each of these three domains and describes areas for future work.

COMPREHENSION INSTRUCTION

Good instruction is the most powerful means of developing proficient comprehenders and preventing reading comprehension problems. Narrowly defined, comprehension instruction promotes the ability to *learn from text*. More broadly, comprehension instruction gives students access to culturally important domains of knowledge and provides a means of pursuing affective and intellectual goals. A major goal for the research agenda we propose is improving classroom instruction in comprehension, both by exploring how to ensure the broader implementation of instructional strategies known to work and by building a research base to inform the design of new instructional paradigms.

Effective teachers of comprehension enact practices that reflect the orchestration of knowledge about readers, texts, purposeful activity, and contexts for the purpose of advancing students' thoughtful, competent, and motivated reading. Instructional decisionmaking is a dynamic and highly interactive process. To illustrate, Chapter Three described the many reader variables that are integral to proficient reading comprehension. Drawing on this literature, we characterize students along a continuum from "low need" to "high need" in terms of the instructional support they will require to become proficient comprehenders. However, this characterization of the reader must also take into account the nature of the text that the student is reading and the nature of the task that is motivating the reader. We argue that any reader can be considered high-need depending on how challenging the text is (i.e., the text is poorly written, dense, or contains a number of unfamiliar ideas) or depending on the way the reader is to demonstrate his or her understanding of the text (e.g., recall, reasoning, application, or evaluation). Finally, the teacher must consider the broad range of contextual factors that influence instructional opportunities for particular learners.

These contextual factors include, but are not limited to, community- and schoolwide factors, the culture of the classroom, the specific curriculum and instructional activities in which students are engaged, and the nature of the interaction between teacher and students as well as among students. Similarly, a student who appears to be a high-need reader when the reader variables are considered in isolation may, in fact, be very successful in an instructional setting in which the teacher attends to this student's needs while selecting texts, designing tasks for him or her, and deciding how to structure the context to best support the student's participation and learning.

To maximize the possibility that research will yield *usable knowledge*, instructional research, regardless of the method employed, needs to attend to each of these elements of reading comprehension. Careful descriptions of both the texts used in the research and the specific nature of the task(s) for which students are using reading in the specific context of instruction need to accompany careful descriptions of the participants. The context includes, but is not limited to (in the case of classroom-based research), general classroom conditions (reported in Pressley et al., 2001) that set the stage for effective instruction, the specific nature of the instructional activity or activities in which the learner is engaged, and the specific nature of the support that teachers, peers, and instructional tools (e.g., computers) provide.

What We Already Know About Comprehension Instruction

The RAND Reading Study Group's prioritization of comprehension instruction set forth in the agenda presented in this chapter is based upon a fairly well-articulated knowledge base.

1.   Instruction that is designed to enhance reading fluency leads to fairly sig-
      nificant gains in word recognition and fluency and to moderate gains in
      comprehension.

A substantial amount of practice over an extended period of time is required for
a reader to acquire fluency. Most fluency instruction consists of the repeated
reading of the same text and uses many techniques. Sometimes the repeated
reading practice is done independently; sometimes the reader is assisted by a
teacher who provides corrective feedback; sometimes the reader listens to the
text before practicing or reads along with a teacher or a tape. Some studies have
incorporated partner reading in which peers, not a teacher, give feedback.

The National Reading Panel (NRP) (2000) examined the wide-ranging literature
on repeated reading. A meta-analysis of 14 studies indicated that the mean
weighted effect size of comparisons of one or another of these techniques
versus a no-instruction control varied depending on what type of outcome
measure was examined. It was largest (.55) when the outcome measure was
word recognition, next largest (.44) with a fluency measure, and smallest (.35)
with a comprehension outcome measure. The NRP found that repeated reading
was effective for normal readers through grade 4 (there were no studies of
normal readers beyond grade 4) and for students with reading problems
throughout high school.

The NRP also examined three other sets of studies: studies looking at the
immediate effect of different programs of repetition and feedback during oral
reading on the reading performance of a specific passage (these studies did not
attempt to assess transfer to uninstructed passages); studies using small groups
of students; and studies that compared the efficacy of two different oral reading
procedures. All three sets of studies corroborated the findings of the meta-
analysis, indicating the value of repeated reading. No conclusions could be
drawn about the relative effectiveness of independent repeated reading and
guided oral reading practice or of any other two procedures, such as reading
with or without feedback. One exception to this conclusion of no differences
comes from a study by Rashotte and Torgesen (1985). They compared passages
that either shared or did not share many words with the outcome measures.
They noted gains when the passages shared words but no gains when the
passages did not share words. This result suggests that very poor readers
probably at least learn words from repeated reading (Faulkner & Levy, 1999).
Most studies have found that reading interconnected text is necessary for
effective fluency instruction, but one recent study (Tan & Nicholson, 1997) has
indicated that reading of isolated word lists also leads to increased fluency.

Several studies have indicated that these repeated-reading techniques are feasible for classroom use (Dixon-Krauss, 1995; Rasinski, 1990). No extensive

preparation is needed to use these techniques successfully (Reutzel & Hollingsworth, 1993). Studies dealing with readers with learning disabilities have found that peer tutoring can be successfully incorporated into the instruction (Mathes & Fuchs, 1993; Simmons et al., 1994).

Other studies have assessed the effect of simple practice in reading, such as Sustained Silent Reading. However, merely encouraging students to read extensively did not result in improved reading, according to the findings of a meta-analysis (NRP, 2000). It is thus not clear whether there are conditions under which practice in reading would promote fluency and comprehension.

Another approach to promoting fluency involves ensuring that proficiency and fluency are acquired during instruction in all components of reading, starting with letter knowledge and phonemic awareness and moving to decoding and word recognition (Berninger, Abbott, Billingsley, & Nagy, in press; Wolf & Katzir-Cohen, 2001). Berninger, Abbott, Brooksher, Lemos, Ogier, Zook, & Mostafapour (in press); and Wolf & Katzir-Cohen (2001) have developed intervention programs that address specific component skills, foster linkages among all relevant systems—orthographic, phonological, semantic, and morphological—and emphasize fluency at each step. These programs are very new, and no data on their success in promoting fluency are currently available.

2.   Instruction can be effective in providing students with a repertoire of strategies that promote comprehension monitoring and foster comprehension.

Because meaning does not exist in text, but rather must be actively constructed, instruction in how to employ strategies is necessary to improve comprehension. To construct meaning, students must monitor their understanding and apply strategic effort. We know that students who are good comprehenders read for a purpose and actively monitor whether that purpose is being met. They notice when something they are reading is incongruous with their background knowledge or is unclear, then they take action to clarify their understanding, such as rereading or reading ahead. They may also stop periodically when reading to summarize what they have read as a way to check their understanding.

To further enhance comprehension, good comprehenders also use strategies that help them retain, organize, and evaluate the information they are reading. Among these strategies is a well-defined set that we know, as a result of rigorous investigation and replication, leads to improved comprehension when employed by readers. This set of strategies includes concept mapping, question generating, question answering, summarizing, and story mapping as delineated in the NRP report (2000). Additional strategies investigated in non-experimental studies that may also prove beneficial to students include mental imagery, knowledge activation, mnemonics, and expository pattern identification.

Judging by the experimental studies reviewed by the NRP (2000), we know that engaging students in identifying the big ideas in a text and in graphically depicting the relationships among these ideas improves their recall and comprehension of text. We also know that in grades 3–5, engaging students in elaborative questioning improves their comprehension of text read during instruction and their comprehension of new text read independently. Similarly, teaching students in grades 3–9 to self-question while reading text enhances their understanding of the text used in the instruction and improves their comprehension of new text. Studies conducted in the upper elementary grades indicate that learning to paraphrase text, identify the gist of a text, and identify and integrate the big ideas in a text enhance the recall of text and the capacity to understand new text. Teaching students in grades 3–6 to identify and represent story structure improves their comprehension of the story they have read. In the case of this strategy, there was no evidence that the strategy transferred to the reading of new stories and improvement was more marked for low-achieving readers.

3.   The explicitness with which teachers teach comprehension strategies makes a difference in learner outcomes, especially for low-achieving students.

Understanding the nature of the reading comprehension problems experienced by many students who are low achieving has helped in developing instructional approaches that enhance the comprehension abilities of these students. An important instructional strategy for these learners consists of making instruction very explicit. Explicit instruction provides a clear explanation of the criterion task, encourages students to pay attention, activates prior knowledge, breaks the task into small steps, provides sufficient practice at every step, and incorporates teacher feedback. It is particularly important for the teacher to model the comprehension strategies being taught. Careful and slow fading of the scaffolding is important.

Sometimes this explicit instruction is helpful for low-achieving students but is superfluous for normal readers (Wong & Jones, 1982). Sometimes improvement occurs not because of the specific strategies being taught but because students have been actively interacting with the texts. This active interaction triggers the use of strategies that inactive learners possess but do not normally use.

Explicit instruction generates the immediate use of comprehension strategies, but there is less evidence that students continue to use the strategies in the classroom and outside of school after instruction ends (Keeny, Cannizzo &

Flavell, 1967; Ringel & Springer, 1980) or that they transfer the strategies to new situations.

Recent studies have underscored the importance of teacher preparation when the goal is to deliver effective instruction in reading comprehension strategies (Duffy et al., 1987; Brown et al., 1996). This is especially important when the students are low performing. Implementing a direct approach to cognitive strategy instruction in the context of the actual classroom has proven problematic. Proficient reading involves much more than using individual strategies. It involves a constant, ongoing adaptation of many cognitive processes. Successful teachers of reading comprehension must respond flexibly and opportunistically to students' needs for instructive feedback as they read. Lengthy, intensive teacher preparation is effective in helping teachers deliver successful strategy instruction that has improved student outcomes on reading comprehension tests.

4.   There are a number of working hypotheses about the role of instruction in explaining and addressing the problems of poor comprehenders.

One of the most vexing problems facing middle and secondary school teachers today is that many students come into their classrooms without the requisite knowledge, skills, and dispositions to read the materials placed before them. These students are, for one reason or another, poor comprehenders. Poor comprehenders are students who can neither read nor demonstrate satisfactory understanding of texts appropriate for their grade level. Many teachers are frustrated by what they see as an ever-increasing number of students who are poor comprehenders.

Instructional research with poor comprehenders has been motivated by a particular set of hypotheses about impediments to comprehension. Some of these hypotheses suggest that the problems of poor comprehenders are an outgrowth of differential instruction; that is, these students have been denied the kinds of instruction that advance reading comprehension. This hypothesis is particularly relevant for students who have a history of reading problems (e.g., decoding problems in grades 1 and 2). For example, McDermott and Varenne (1995) documented that teachers working with high-achieving students focused on higher-order thinking with text and communicated clearly that the purpose of reading was understanding. In contrast, these same teachers, when working with low-achieving students, focused on low-level factual reading, interrupted children's reading more frequently than their errors would justify (see also Shake, 1986), and communicated little about comprehension as the goal of reading. A corollary to this hypothesis is that students with a history of reading challenges read less text; hence, they accrue less background knowledge to bring to the reading of new text.

Research has indicated, however, that specific instruction, for example, pre-reading, can improve poor comprehenders' understanding of a difficult text. Researchers have used instructional scripts that provide students with essential background knowledge, key concepts, and vocabulary (Graves, Cooke, & LaBerge, 1983) or have activated students' background knowledge through extended discussions (Langer, 1984). Researchers have also used such activities as story structures or graphic organizers to provide scaffolding for improved comprehension of a selected text (NRP, 2000). Pre- and post-writing activities have also been used as effective instructional activities to promote comprehension for low-achieving readers. These instructional activities effectively address the problem of poor comprehension by providing this sort of instructional scaffolding to help low-achieving readers comprehend texts above their independent reading level.

In addition, poor comprehenders can be guided to effectively employ a number of strategies to improve their understanding of text. For example, researchers have helped poor comprehenders draw inferences by using a pre-reading strategy in which they activate attention and prior knowledge or by using particular strategies in the course of reading, such as restating information from the text (Chan et al., 1987; Idol-Maestas, 1985; Schumaker et al., 1982).

The nature of the strategy taught seems less significant than the role that strategy instruction plays in engaging the reader in active interaction with the text (Chan & Cole, 1986). A synthesis of the research literature on teaching comprehension strategies to students with learning problems (Gersten, Fuchs, Williams, & Baker, in press) indicates that successful comprehension instruction for the poor comprehender is characterized by explicit modeling by the teacher, additional opportunities for practice with feedback, skillful adjustments to the learner's level, and the reader's mindful engagement with the purposes for reading.

5. The role of vocabulary instruction in enhancing comprehension is complex.

As we described earlier in this report, vocabulary knowledge is strongly linked to reading comprehension (Freebody & Anderson, 1983), and there is reason to believe that vocabulary knowledge is an especially important factor in understanding the reading problems experienced by second-language learners (García, 1991; Laufer & Sim, 1985). However, this relationship between vocabulary knowledge and comprehension is extremely complex, confounded, as it is, by the complexity of relationships among vocabulary knowledge, conceptual and cultural knowledge, and instructional opportunities.

These complexities speak to the unique and significant role that instructional research can play in enhancing the education field's understanding of the role of vocabulary knowledge in comprehension. The NRP (2000) found that direct instruction of vocabulary improved reading comprehension. The effects of extensive reading on vocabulary growth are, however, debatable. The NRP did not find compelling evidence that programs that are designed to increase independent reading, such as Sustained Silent Reading, promoted vocabulary growth. Nevertheless, there is a powerful correlational relationship between the volume of reading and vocabulary growth among first-language learners (Stanovich & Cunningham, 1992), and "book-flood" studies (in which children are provided with numerous books for use at school or at home) with second-language learners have shown powerful effects (Elley, 1991). Further, a wealth of evidence relates children's oral language experiences to subsequent vocabulary growth (Dickinson & Tabors, 2001). Much of this evidence comes from studies of the effects of homes and preschools on language development. Less is known about the effects of school-based oral language activities and vocabulary learning and growth, although Meichenbaum and Biemiller (1998), among others, have argued that the fourth-grade slump cited earlier in this report is caused, at least in part, by the failure of schools to promote oral language development while children are still working on the mechanics of reading.

Much of the instructional research in vocabulary has been designed to document, or compare, the effectiveness of different methods of teaching individual words. Although some generalizations can be made about the characteristics of effective vocabulary instruction (Stahl & Fairbanks, 1986), the number of studies that have directly examined the effects of vocabulary instruction on reading comprehension is still relatively small. Some of the strongest demonstrations of the effects of vocabulary instruction on reading comprehension—the work of Beck and her colleagues (e.g., Beck, Perfetti, & McKeown, 1982; McKeown, Beck, Omanson, & Pople, 1985)—used rather artificial texts heavily loaded with unfamiliar words. Little, if any, research addresses the question of which conditions—the types of texts, words, readers, and outcomes—can actually improve comprehension.

Effective vocabulary instruction presupposes choosing the right words to teach. This is another area in which more research is needed. How does a teacher choose which words to teach? What are the instructionally relevant subcategories of words? Graves (2000) and others have suggested some distinctions that must be considered, such as the difference between teaching new concepts and teaching new labels for familiar concepts, or the difference between teaching students to recognize in print words already in their oral vocabularies and teaching them words not yet in their reading or oral vocabularies. Nation (1989; Laufer & Nation, 1999) has offered another instructionally relevant way to categorize words—as high-frequency words, domain-specific technical vocabulary, low-frequency words, or high-utility academic vocabulary. Although such distinctions are undoubtedly crucial in making instructional decisions, there is still little documentation of how well teachers can use such categories or of the actual effect of such categories on the effectiveness of vocabulary instruction.

Some vocabulary researchers (e.g., Laufer & Sim, 1985) have stressed the importance of high-frequency words for learners of English, because a relatively small number of words constitute the bulk of words encountered in text. However, the most effective methodology for teaching high-frequency words still needs to be explored, given that such words are also the most likely to have multiple meanings. Others have stressed the importance of focusing on words intermediate in frequency—not so frequent that they are already known by almost everyone, yet frequent enough to be worth teaching. Much remains to be learned about identifying these words and about the effectiveness of instructional approaches that focus on such words. Another dimension of choosing words for instruction has to do with the relationships among instructed words. Materials for learners of English as a second language often group words on the basis of meaning. However, some evidence suggests that teaching words in groups that are highly similar in meaning is a hindrance, rather than an aid, to learning (Tinkham, 1993; Waring, 1997).

Teaching individual words presupposes some sort of explanation of their meanings, which is most likely to be in the form of a definition. Although some research has explored the effectiveness of different types of definitions (Fischer, 1994; McKeown, 1993; Scott & Nagy, 1997), relatively little is known about this area. To our knowledge, for example, no one has explored the question of whether different types of definitions are appropriate for different types of words or for different stages of word learning (e.g., initial exposure versus consolidation and refinement of word knowledge). Research could help illuminate what knowledge, skills, and abilities best allow learners to benefit from definitions or, more generally, from vocabulary instruction (e.g., dictionary skills, metalinguistic abilities, language proficiency levels). There is little question that one component of proficient comprehension is the ability to cope with any unfamiliar words encountered during reading. Readers need to be able to use the information provided by context, by morphology (word parts), and by dictionaries or other reference materials and to coordinate information from these sources.

In a recent meta-analysis, Fukkink and de Glopper (1998) found that instruction in the use of context improved students' ability to use contextual clues to figure out word meanings. However, on the basis of a similar meta-analysis, Kuhn and Stahl (1998) argued that such instruction was not demonstrably more effective than simple practice. Instruction in the use of morphology and definitions has been less thoroughly investigated than instruction in the use of context. The possibility of online dictionaries and other word-learning aids opens up additional areas for research.

The effectiveness of context for second-language learners is still a matter of debate. A variety of evidence indicates that second-language learners have more difficulty using context than do native-language learners (e.g., Nagy, McClure, & Montserrat, 1997). However, second-language learners who face the task of simply learning new labels rather than learning new concepts may be at a relative advantage.

Research is also needed on what makes some students more effective independent word learners than others. Some of the contributing factors, such as language proficiency and existing vocabulary and background knowledge, are obvious. Phonological processing ability contributes to vocabulary learning, especially for second-language learners (Eviatar & Ibrahim, 2000; Muter & Diethelm, 2001). It also seems likely that a variety of metalinguistic abilities contribute to vocabulary learning (Nagy & Scott, 2000).

A number of vocabulary researchers have expressed the opinion that "word consciousness" or "word awareness" may be an important element in promoting vocabulary growth (Graves, Watts-Taffe, & Graves, 1998). As yet, no research has measured such a construct, let alone documented its effect on vocabulary learning. One reason that word consciousness and its effects on vocabulary growth are not well understood is that various constructs could fall under this heading but they are not all necessarily related to one another. For example, the concept of words (Roberts, 1992), morphological awareness (Anglin, 1993; Carlisle, 1995), word schemas (Nagy & Scott, 1990), word play, and an appreciation for effective word choice (Scott & Nagy, 1997) could all fall under the term *word consciousness*. Little is known, however, about how these constructs relate to one another or to vocabulary growth.

Various aspects of word consciousness may be crucial to strategies for independent word learning. Morphological awareness is undoubtedly involved in using word parts to make inferences about the meanings of new words. Word schemas—knowledge of what might constitute a possible meaning for a word—could be an important part of making inferences about new words encountered in context (Nagy & Scott, 1990) and may also contribute to the effective use of definitions. For example, Fischer (1994) speculates that one factor limiting the effectiveness of second-language learners' use of bilingual dictionaries is the expectation that there will be one-to-one mappings between the meanings of words in two languages.

For speakers of Spanish who are learning English (or vice versa), a specific type of word awareness—awareness of cognate relationships—may be especially important. Many words in the vocabulary of literate or academic English are similar in both form and meaning to everyday Spanish words (e.g., *tranquil/tranquilo* and *pensive/pensivo*). Bilingual students differ in their ability to recognize such relationships (Nagy, García, Durgunoglu, & Hancin-Bhatt, 1993; García & Nagy, 1993), and the ability to recognize such relationships appears to be associated with more effective reading strategies (Jiménez, García, & Pearson, 1996).

Each of the four components of a vocabulary curriculum outlined by Graves (2000)—teaching individual words, encouraging wide reading, teaching word-learning strategies, and promoting word consciousness—is likely to make an important contribution to students' long-term vocabulary growth and, hence, to their reading comprehension. However, in addition to our incomplete knowledge about each component, we know extremely little about their relative contribution and how they interact with one another.

6. Teachers who provide comprehension strategy instruction that is deeply connected within the context of subject matter learning, such as history and science, foster comprehension development.

As we described earlier in this chapter, the NRP evidence suggests that teaching such reading strategies as questioning, summarizing, comprehension monitoring, and using graphic organizers facilitates reading comprehension. Several quasi-experimental investigations show that when the strategy instruction is fully embedded in in-depth learning of content, the strategies are learned to a high level of competence (Guthrie, Van Meter, Hancock, Alao, Anderson, & McCann, 1998). If students learn that strategies are tools for understanding the conceptual content of text, then the strategies become purposeful and integral to reading activities. Connecting cognitive strategies to students' growing knowledge of a content area enables students to both increase their awareness of and deliberately use the strategies as means for learning (Brown, 1997) in microgenetic analyses of instruction. Unless the strategies are closely linked with knowledge and understanding in a content area, students are unlikely to learn the strategies fully, may not perceive the strategies as valuable tools, and are less likely to use them in new learning situations with new text.

Integrating strategy instruction into content domains requires a balance. The priority of instructing for reading comprehension must be balanced with the priority of teaching the content area itself. Teachers can help students learn that gaining new ideas, increased understanding, and literary experience is an aim of reading and that strategies are a powerful way to accomplish that aim. This information helps students use strategies reliably when they are appropriate. If comprehension strategies are taught with an array of content and a range of texts that are too wide, then students will not fully learn them. If strategies are taught with too narrow a base of content or text, then students do not have a chance to learn how to transfer them to new reading situations (Rosenshine & Meister, 1994). The optimal balance enables students to learn that strategies are an important means for understanding but are not the main point of reading activities. The main purposes for reading are gaining meaning and gaining knowledge.

An important aspect of strategy development is to enable students to become self-initiating (Alexander & Murphy, 1998), according to several reviews of empirical literature. Students who spontaneously apply a strategy, such as questioning, when it is sensible will improve their comprehension. Thus, to be effective comprehenders, students must have motivation, self-efficacy, and ownership regarding their purposes for reading and their strategies. Teaching strategies integrated with content enables students to become proficient, self-regulating strategy users.

7.   Using various genres of text (i.e., narrative and informational text) diversifies instructional opportunities, as assessed by teacher and student discourse.

A knowledge of text structure is an important factor in fostering comprehension. Students with some knowledge of text structure expect texts to unfold in certain ways. Even before they enter school, children have a rudimentary sense of narrative structure. The first texts they are introduced to in school are narrative in structure, which allows an easy transition from oral to written language (Van Dongen & Westby, 1986). In school, children are also introduced to expository text, which is more complex, diverse, and challenging.

Readers who are unaware of structure do not approach a text with any particular plan of action (Meyer, Brandt, & Bluth, 1980). Consequently, they tend to retrieve information in a seemingly random way. Students who are aware of text structure organize the text as they read, and they recognize and retain the important information it contains.

Simple exposure to stories is helpful, but explicit instruction is valuable. Children are taught to ask themselves generic questions that focus on the principal components of a story, which helps them identify the relevant and important information in stories (Mandler & Johnson, 1977; Stein & Glenn, 1979; Williams, 1993). In addition to their value as an organizational guide to the text structure, the questions enhance the active processing of the text, thus qualifying the generic questions as comprehension-monitoring instruction. Such instruction improves students' ability to see relationships in stories, answer comprehension questions, and retell the stories in a focused fashion. The positive effects of an intervention are most likely to accrue on measures closely aligned with the specific instruction provided. The effect of interventions that teach the use of text structure is not as strong on transfer measures. Although stories constitute the bulk of reading material for instruction in the early grades, a case for greater inclusion of other text genres has been made (Duke, 2000; Pappas & Barry, 1997). Such inclusion will allow instruction that more closely matches the demands of reading in later grades.

As readers progress through school, the demands placed on them change. At about grade 4, they are expected to read expository material in content instruction. Because expository text is often dense with information and unfamiliar technical vocabulary, students must perform complex cognitive tasks to extract and synthesize its content (Lapp, Flood, & Ranck-Buhr, 1995). Expository text involves relatively long passages, less familiar content, and more complex and varied structures (Armbruster & Anderson, 1984). Explicit teaching about structure enables students to differentiate among common structures and to identify the important information in a text in a coherent, organized way (Armbruster & Armstrong, 1993).

Various instructional techniques have been used to help students comprehend expository text, including teaching them to use generic questions to self-question (Wong & Jones, 1982), to use mapping to analyze the text (Swanson, Kozleski, & Stegink, 1987; Boyle & Weishaar, 1997), to summarize (Nelson, Smith, & Dodd, 1992), and to employ other simple strategies. These interventions were effective.

A body of research exists on methods for adapting or modifying texts (e.g., Beck, McKeown, Sinatra, & Loxterman, 1991) to make them easier to comprehend. This literature is important, but it does not address the issue of helping students understand the texts they may encounter in their content area classes and on high-stakes tests.

8. Teachers who give students choices, challenging tasks, and collaborative learning structures increase their motivation to read and comprehend text.

For students from grade 1 to grade 12, classroom activities that enable and encourage them to take responsibility for their reading increase their reading achievement. For example, extensive observations of classroom instruction for primary students show that when teachers provide challenging passages for reading, students exert effort and persistence. And when students have a limited, but meaningful, choice about the learning activity, such as which part of a text to read, they invest greater energy in learning than when the tasks are always prescribed by the teacher (Turner, 1995).

With elementary and middle school students, quasi-experimental and structural equation modeling studies have shown that teachers who provide meaningful choices and autonomy increase students' motivation to read and to expend effort to gain knowledge from text (Reeve, Bolt, & Cai, 1999). The explanation for the benefit of autonomy support for reading comprehension is that students become more-active learners when teachers provide a minimal, but meaningful, choice in the topics, texts, activities, and strategies for learning. For example, when given a choice of two books for a comprehension activity, students will choose the one that interests them. This interest deepens the students' thinking and their use of strategies and background knowledge during reading (see Schiefele, 1999, for a review of experimental evidence). High interest, derived from choice, leads to high comprehension.

The roles of motivation and engagement as links between instruction and achievement have been documented by many investigators (Skinner, Wellborn, & Connell, 1990; see Guthrie & Wigfield, 2000, for a review of empirical research). In brief, the most predictive statistical models show that engagement is a mediator of the effects of instruction on reading achievement. If instruction increases students' engagement, then students' achievement increases. In this literature, engagement refers to a combination of the following: (a) the use of cognitive strategies; (b) the presence of an intrinsic motivation to read; (c) the use of background knowledge to understand text; and (d) the social interchanges in reading, such as discussing the meaning of a paragraph or the theme of a narrative. Therefore, instruction affects reading comprehension outcomes through the avenue of active engagement in frequent, thoughtful reading for understanding.

9.   Effective teachers enact a wide range of instructional practices that they use thoughtfully and dynamically.

Most people do not realize how complex teaching is. Effective teachers do more than teach specific strategies or make available to students a wide variety of texts. Indeed, effective teachers of reading engage in a diverse array of instructional practices (NRP, 2000; Pressley et al., 2001; Taylor, Pearson, Clark, & Walpole, 1999). This panoply of practices results in a complex environment in which comprehension can be fostered.

A review of studies of effective teachers reveals some of these important instructional practices and activities. For example, effective teachers establish a complex set of organizational and management routines in their classrooms, which they use to ensure a minimal amount of disruption and a maximal amount of time-on-task. Indeed, almost all of the time in the classrooms of effective teachers is spent on instruction. In addition, effective teachers provide an atmosphere of support and encouragement. In their classrooms, readers feel comfortable taking risks and are expected to achieve.

Effective teachers also use a variety of instructional practices that relate more specifically to reading comprehension. For example, effective teachers ask high-level comprehension questions that require students to make inferences and to think beyond the text. Effective teachers help readers make connections between texts they read and their personal lives and experiences. Effective teachers use small-group instruction to meet the individual needs of their readers. Effective teachers provide their readers with practice reading materials at their appropriate reading level. Effective teachers of young readers monitor progress in reading by using informal assessments.

One critically important, but thorny, aspect of teaching reading in general and comprehension in particular is the appropriate balance between teaching skills and using literature. Over the last 20 years, the reading field has vacillated between the two—with fierce opposition between those recommending one or the other. However, the choice does not seem to concern most teachers. In a survey of teacher practices, Baumann, Hoffman, Moon, and Duffy-Hester (1998) reported that teachers believed both to be essential for good teaching. In fact, teachers reported that they taught skills *and* extensively used literature.

10. Despite the well-developed knowledge base supporting the value of instruction designed to enhance comprehension, comprehension instruction continues to receive inadequate time and attention in typical classroom instruction across the primary and upper elementary grades.

In the late 1970s, research revealed that teachers devoted only 2 percent of the classroom time designated for reading instruction to actually teaching students how to comprehend what they read (Durkin, 1978–79). Twenty years later not much has changed in the upper elementary (Pressley, 2000) or primary grades (Taylor et al., 1999). For example, Taylor and colleagues documented the limited opportunities that children in grades K–3 had to develop knowledge and thinking even in the context of schools that were effectively "beating the odds"—that is, schools that were realizing higher early reading achievement gains than would be predicted given the demographics of their student populations. Using survey and classroom observation data, they reported that only 16 percent of the teachers in the entire sample emphasized comprehension.

Despite the hypothesized role that inexperience with informational text plays in the fourth-grade slump (Chall, Jacobs, & Baldwin, 1990), and despite evidence that some young children prefer to read informational text (Pappas & Barry, 1997), primary-grade classrooms have a significant dearth of informational texts (Duke, 2000). Beginning in grade 4 and throughout their formal education, students will spend the majority of their time reading expository text, yet instruction in grades 1–3 primarily uses narrative text. Recently a plethora of engaging informational texts, written for primary-grade students, has become available. However, these books are not yet in sufficient supply in primary classrooms, and primary-grade teachers have not yet balanced teaching reading for informational and narrative texts.

What We Need to Know About Comprehension Instruction

What specific issues of educational urgency exist, and how can we formulate the most promising research directions for addressing them? We start with four problem statements related to low-achieving students and one concerning second-language readers, then turn to issues of instructional design relevant to the entire student population.

1.   For poor comprehenders in the general education setting, would focusing more time on comprehension instruction while using currently available curricula and instructional strategies generate adequate gains?

Studies of classroom practice are unanimous in noting the scarcity of time devoted to comprehension instruction. Neither in the primary grades, when the focus of reading instruction is typically word reading, nor in the middle elementary grades do teachers spend much time helping students learn how to approach complex texts strategically. Although the current approaches to teaching comprehension are neither adequately rich nor research-based, the possibility exists that they are adequate to address comprehension problems for some learners, if sufficient time is devoted to instruction.

2.   For poor comprehenders in the general education setting, how should time and instructional emphasis be allocated among (a) promoting fluency, (b) teaching vocabulary, (c) instructing students in the use of reading strategies, (d) providing extensive reading of informational and literary text, (e) encouraging writing based on reading, (f) using multimedia to support content learning, and (g) using computer programs to improve reading skills?

Some evidence supports the efficacy of promoting fluency, teaching vocabulary, teaching strategies, promoting wide reading, and encouraging writing based on reading in promoting comprehension. In contrast, little evidence supports the efficacy of using multimedia for content learning or computer programs for skill development, but these practices are widely implemented. Teachers need guidance, which is totally absent in the available research literature, about how to combine and prioritize these various instructional approaches in the classroom.

3.   How do teachers identified as effective with low achievers create, administer, and use reading assessments that are related to curricular goals and useful for informing instruction across grade levels and across diverse populations of students? Further, how do effective teachers determine the

knowledge, skills, and dispositions that diverse readers bring to reading activities?

Studies of effective teachers have been informative about aspects of instruction that work well to improve comprehension. We know little, though, about effective teachers' selection, use, and interpretation of assessments to inform their practice. Such practice-based wisdom, if it is indeed available, could be useful if verified and disseminated more widely.

4. For low-achieving students in high-poverty schools, what organization of instructional practices is beneficial: (a) instruction in word recognition and fluency, (b) access to and use of an abundance of content and literary texts, (c) explicit teaching of reading strategies, (d) explicit teaching of vocabulary and the use of vocabulary knowledge in reading, (e) out-of-school literacy pursuits to enhance reading development, (f) writing based on reading, and (g) opportunities for multimedia links to support reading and writing tasks?

As noted above, little evidence supports the efficacy of giving instruction in word recognition and fluency, teaching vocabulary, teaching strategies, promoting wide reading, and encouraging writing based on reading in promoting comprehension. Also, there is little evidence concerning the efficacy of computer programs for skill development or of out-of-school literacy supports, but these practices seem promising. Teachers working in high-poverty schools need guidance on how to combine and prioritize various instructional approaches in the classroom. In particular, they need to learn how to teach comprehension while attending to the often poor word-reading skills their students bring to the middle and later elementary grades.

5. For students who are learning English as a second language, how should time and instructional emphasis be allocated among (a) giving instruction in word recognition and fluency, (b) teaching vocabulary, (c) instructing about strategies, (d) providing extensive reading of informational and literary text, (e) encouraging writing based on reading, (f) using multimedia to support content learning, (g) using of out-of-school literacy pursuits to enhance reading development, and (h) using computer programs to improve reading skills?

Teachers of English-language learners, like teachers of poor comprehenders in the general education setting and teachers working in high-poverty schools, have available a number of instructional techniques and strategies that research has shown to be effective and additional techniques that are endorsed by the wisdom of practice. However, selecting among these various instructional practices for particular students and groups of students and devoting appropriate amounts of time to using the practices remain a challenge. And research offers little guidance.

6.   Under what conditions does instruction about strategies to improve reading comprehension actually lead to students' using the strategic approaches for various texts and tasks in diverse contexts and at different age levels? What specific instructional activities, materials, and practices are related to effective comprehension and to the engagement of students from various cultural and linguistic backgrounds at varying grade levels?

It is well documented (NRP, 2000) that students can be taught to use strategies to advance their ability and inclination to independently learn from text.[1] Furthermore, evidence suggests that a relatively small set of strategies appears to be consistently effective across diverse populations of students, with diverse forms of text, and for diverse tasks that the reader is to accomplish. Finally, and perhaps most important, there is evidence that the power of strategy instruction is the extent to which strategies are taught in the service of interpreting text, not as ends in and of themselves. But this robust knowledge base is still incomplete.

7.   How can excellent, direct comprehension instruction be embedded in content instruction that uses inquiry-based methods and authentic reading materials?

Contemporary national benchmarks in science call for instruction to be inquiry-based. The standards in history call for students to learn the practices of historical analysis, including the use of primary documents. Contemporary language arts standards call for students, at all ages, to read authentic literature across genres (e.g., novels, memoirs, interviews) and to write in various genres. Web-based technology affords students the opportunity to access numerous sources of information. All of these opportunities provide potentially powerful contexts in which students can learn to interpret text and can learn how to learn from text. However, with the exception of a few studies (Brown & Campione, 1994; Guthrie, et al., 1998), we know little about how these instructional contexts lead to improved reading comprehension or about how specific teacher practices in these contexts can lead to improved comprehension. Specifically:

- What is the role of direct instruction in specific comprehension-monitoring and comprehension-fostering strategies in an inquiry-focused learning environment?

---

[1]This statement applies to upper elementary through adult education. We have a much leaner knowledge base regarding strategy instruction in the preschool and primary grades.

- How can activities that are designed to promote knowledge-building be extended to enhance self-regulated reading?

- What role does experience with a diverse array of texts, used in the context of subject-matter learning, play in promoting thoughtful, competent, and motivated readers?

8.   How do we ensure that all children know the vocabulary they will encounter in content area and advanced texts?

A number of significant researchable issues are related to the role of vocabulary in enhancing comprehension. We focus here on four subsets: (a) selecting the words to teach, (b) teaching strategies for learning words independently, (c) fostering word consciousness, and (d) examining the interplay between different components of a vocabulary curriculum. (See Appendix A for a specific description of these issues.)

9.   How do national, state, and local policies and practices facilitate or impede the efforts of teachers to implement effective comprehension instruction?

The policy literature and teacher journals are filled with examples of how policy changes improved or undermined educational effectiveness. There are notable examples of successfully implemented policies imposed or encouraged by districts and states that changed instructional practices in the domain of word reading. However, a systematic analysis of the effect of these and other policies on comprehension instruction has not been undertaken.

TEACHER EDUCATION AND PROFESSIONAL DEVELOPMENT IN READING COMPREHENSION

An important goal of research on reading comprehension is the larger goal of improving students' reading proficiency. This goal, however, is mediated by at least two critical variables. First, the research must be translated into appropriate *instruction*. Second, *teachers* must enact that instruction. Regardless of the quantity and quality of research-based knowledge about comprehension, unless teachers use that knowledge to improve their instruction, students' reading achievement will not improve. In other words, as Sykes (1999) argued, recent advances in research-based best practices have an effect only to the extent that teachers adopt those practices.

There is reason to question whether teachers use research-based best practices to teach comprehension or other subject areas. Cuban (1993) has argued that, in general, although teachers have made some changes in their classrooms over the last 100 years, the basic forms of instruction have not changed. The recent Third International Math & Science Study (TIMSS) Videotape Classroom Study

(Stigler, Gonzales, Kawanaka, Knoll, & Serrano, 1999) corroborated Cuban's observations and conclusions. In the TIMSS study, researchers found that most American teachers, even those who say they use reform models, still teach using traditional practices. Hiebert and Martin (2001) showed that teachers distort much knowledge about mathematics reform to make it consistent with their existing practices. These researchers found that true changes in teaching practice based on research were rare among American teachers.

Whereas some researchers have questioned the extent to which teachers use research-based best practices in their instruction, other researchers have pointed to teacher quality as one of the most critical variables in student achievement. Teacher quality is defined in many ways, from advanced degrees to deep subject matter knowledge to deep pedagogical knowledge (Shulman, 1986). Whatever way it is defined, it is clear that the expertise of the teacher matters, and it matters a lot. In an extensive review of the research on teacher quality and student achievement, Darling-Hammond (2000) found that teacher quality and expertise consistently and accurately predicted student achievement. Additionally, Sykes (1999) pointed to the rather weak effects of efforts at systemic reform without adequate professional development. Sykes argued that early systemic reform efforts—focused on new assessments, new curriculum frameworks, and teaching standards—are not enough to improve student achievement. Research has demonstrated that these efforts need to be accompanied by strong professional development. More-recent systemic reform efforts have focused squarely on the teacher as the center of reform.

One particularly puzzling aspect of school reform is that despite the key role ascribed to teachers when explaining why reforms fail (Cohen & Ball, 1990; Cremin, 1965; Darling-Hammond, 1990), we continue to craft fairly minimal roles for teachers in conceptualizing and enacting reform. The minimal role of the teacher is also vexing when we consider the findings on factors affecting student achievement. Although 48 percent of the variance in student achievement is attributable to home and family factors that are largely out of the school system's control, 51 percent of the variance is attributable to controllable factors, 43 percent of which can be attributed to teacher quality (Ferguson, 1991). Despite these findings, we seem to have few ideas about how to enlist the support of teachers in reform efforts, how to enhance their capacity to maximally contribute to the reform effort, and how to engage teachers in reshaping reform efforts in response to their experiences in enacting reform.

Fullan (1992) reported that the time spent in deliberating on and enacting new educational policies has generally been three times greater than the average time allotted for planning the initial implementation. One hypothesis for this finding might be that we know very little about how to structure and support such a planning process.

Many policymakers have identified the critical role of the teacher in the reform process. "Teachers are, in one sense, the problem that policy seeks to correct" (Cohen & Ball, 1990, p. 238). Underinvestment in teacher knowledge has killed many a reform movement in the past, especially those that strove toward child-centered forms of education (Darling-Hammond, 1990). Cremin (1965) attributes the past failures of educational reform efforts to teacher capacity. The landmark research reported in the special issue of *Educational Evaluation and Policy Analysis* devoted to teachers' responses to the California mathematics reforms was enormously helpful to our getting a finer sense of the role of the teacher in mediating the change process. The direct study of how innovations affected teaching practices across five elementary teachers' classrooms revealed the varied responses that these teachers made as a function of their knowledge and beliefs. In addition, this research illustrated the ways in which teachers filled in the gaps in their understanding of the policy, creating a melange of practices.

Thus, the teacher must be front and center as we discuss how to improve comprehension instruction in schools today. The question becomes, *How can we bring about increased teacher quality and expertise in teaching reading comprehension?* Teachers who exhibit increased teacher quality and expertise have a deep knowledge about the reading process and reading comprehension. They also have the knowledge and skills to implement research-based instructional strategies in their teaching, ideally while also making their practice-based reflections on those instructional strategies available to researchers. In this report, we identify what we know about the answer to this question and raise new questions for additional research.

To answer this question, we look at two bodies of research: one on teacher education and another on professional development. Teacher education or teacher preparation programs refer to four- and five-year programs (both undergraduate and graduate) whose goal is to prepare individuals for teacher certification. Professional development refers to the ongoing education of certified teachers. We limit our discussion to teacher education and professional development that directly relate to learning how to teach reading comprehension, even though we draw from the larger educational research base in order to answer our question. And we acknowledge in advance that the research base on effective teacher education and professional development is disappointingly thin. Nonetheless, we argue that it is sufficient to support doing a better job than we are now doing, even as we pursue research designed to provide enhanced content about excellent comprehension instruction and about improved models for teacher education and professional development.

What We Already Know About Teacher Preparation

A common belief among many Americans is that teaching is something that people can do without much preparation (Darling-Hammond & Green, 1994). The need for teacher preparation programs has always been suspect. In fact, during the 1990s, many alternative teacher education programs were developed to certify teachers without requiring traditional teacher preparation. These programs were based in the belief that individuals with extensive life experiences and expertise in a particular domain—science, history, physics, math—could certainly teach in that domain with minimal preparation.

Although this trend has continued over the past 10 years, a plethora of literature related to teacher preparation programs has become available (for the most recent review of this work, see Sikula, 1996). Most of this literature, however, consists of descriptions and discussions of existing teacher preparation programs, case study analyses of pre-service teachers' beliefs and experiences, and recommendations for improving teacher preparation programs that are based on theory, logic, or experience. In addition, the literature is largely descriptive and qualitative (for a recent review of this work applied to reading education, see Fisher, Fox, & Paille, 1996). Although this body of work can be helpful in identifying issues and constructs for future study, it cannot, by itself, be used to make legitimate claims about teacher education programs. In fact, the NRP (2000) found no studies that measured student achievement as a result of teacher education. As Anders and her colleagues (Anders, Hoffman, & Duffy, 2000) stated, "Few . . . claims [about teacher education and reading] stand on a solid research base" (p. 727).

Nevertheless, we do know a few things about teacher preparation programs. For example, we know that pre-service teachers often enter teaching programs with firmly held beliefs about the nature of knowledge and the nature of teaching. These beliefs have been acquired through their own experiences as learners in schools. These beliefs shape how they view the teaching and learning processes and their own teaching and learning. We also know that many pre-service teachers enter teaching with the idea that there is "little need to obtain a knowledge base in pedagogy in order to become effective teachers" (Lanier & Little, 1986, p. 11). In the past, these candidate teachers have viewed education courses as weak and easy courses, the "Mickey Mouse" courses of the university. NRP (2000) found, however, that pre-service teacher education programs appear to improve candidate teachers' knowledge about teaching and learning; pre-service teachers, in other words, learn what they are taught. Thus it is reasonable to conclude that well-designed teacher education programs have a positive effect on reading outcomes.

What We Need to Know About Teacher Preparation

These claims leave much work to be done before we can better understand the effect of teacher preparation programs on developing expertise in teaching reading comprehension. Several key questions need to be addressed:

- What knowledge base (e.g., in language development, sociolinguistics, multiculturalism, reading development) do teachers need for effective reading comprehension instruction?

- What is the relative power of various instructional delivery systems (e.g., field-based experiences, video-based cases, demonstration teaching, microteaching) for helping teachers acquire the knowledge and skills they need to successfully teach comprehension to students of different ages and in different contexts?

- What do extant national data sets (e.g., NAEP) show about the extent to which teacher preparation experiences relate to teacher practices and student performances on comprehension measures?

What We Already Know About Teacher Professional Development

Conventional wisdom among teacher educators is that pre-service teachers are easier to work with than practicing teachers. Although pre-service teachers certainly hold prior beliefs about teaching and learning, these teacher educators think that the beliefs of practicing teachers are typically more entrenched. Many believe that practicing teachers, through their teaching experiences and classroom routines, have developed established ways of thinking about and implementing instruction—ways that are often resistant to change. For example, it is very difficult for practicing teachers to learn how to use instructional strategies that are different from the ones with which they are familiar. Joyce and Showers (1996) found that it takes as many as 30 instances of practicing a new routine before teachers can successfully incorporate it into their repertoire of practice.

Other research has corroborated this conventional wisdom. A body of research demonstrates the ineffectiveness of many traditional forms of in-service education for teachers (Cochran-Smith & Lytle, 1999). First, we know that the traditional staff development format is a relatively brief "one shot" workshop in which a presenter presents information to teachers about instructional practices. The effectiveness of these workshops, when evaluated at all, is typically measured through surveys of teacher satisfaction and only rarely by changes in teacher behavior. For the most part, teachers report that they perceive professional development in general to be of little use or value.

What We Need to Know About Teacher Professional Development

But what conditions promote effective professional development experiences? Effective professional development is associated with several characteristics (NRP, 2000). First, effective programs cover longer periods of time than do less-effective programs. Second, extensive investment of both money and time is needed on a continual basis for effective professional development. Third, effective professional development is content-focused and provides teachers with theoretical understandings of subject matter (Darling-Hammond, 2000; Elmore, 1999–2000; Joyce & Showers, 1996). Finally, a wide variety of content, when used for professional development, appears to be successful (NRP, 2000).

Since most of these claims about professional development in general relate to professional development to improve reading instruction as well, we can use the claims to identify what we do not know about effective professional development that supports high-level reading comprehension instruction. Among the things we need to know are the following:

- What content (declarative and procedural knowledge about readers, text, tasks, and contexts) and sequencing of content lead to effective professional development programs?

- How do various instructional delivery systems for professional development (e.g., in-class coaching, participatory learning, video-based cases, demonstration teaching, collaborative planning, lesson studies) influence the acquisition of knowledge and skills that lead teachers to enact effective instructional practices for students of different ages and in different contexts?

- What are the critical components of professional development that lead to effective instruction and sustained change in teachers' practice?

- How do teachers' existing beliefs and instructional practices influence how teachers use new information about teaching reading when that new information conflicts with what they already believe and do?

- What are various ways to support teachers so that they are willing to spend the time and cognitive effort and energy necessary to improve their comprehension instruction?

ASSESSMENT OF READING COMPREHENSION

Understanding the nature of the problem of reading comprehension requires having available good data identifying which readers can successfully undertake which activities with which texts. Such data are not available, in part because the widely used comprehension assessments are inadequate. Further, the improvement of instruction relies crucially on the availability of information about the effectiveness of instruction. Teachers need reliable and valid assessments tied closely to their curricula so that they can see which students are learning as expected and which need extra help. In addition, schools, districts, and states are increasingly calling for reliable and valid assessments that reflect progress toward general benchmarks of reading, writing, and mathematics ability. For the area of reading comprehension, good assessments that are tied to curriculum as well as good assessments of general comprehension capacity are sorely needed. These assessments need to be constructed in accordance with the many advances in psychometric theory.

What We Already Know About Comprehension Assessments

Currently available assessments in the field of reading comprehension generate persistent complaints that these instruments

- inadequately represent the complexity of the target domain

- conflate comprehension with vocabulary, domain-specific knowledge, word reading ability, and other reader capacities involved in comprehension

- do not rest on an understanding of reading comprehension as a developmental process or as a product of instruction

- do not examine the assumptions underlying the relationship of successful performance to the dominant group's interests and values

- are not useful for teachers

- tend to narrow the curriculum

- are unidimensional and method-dependent, often failing to address even minimal criteria for reliability and validity.

Indeed, most currently used comprehension assessments reflect the purpose for which they were originally developed—to sort children on a single dimension by using a single method. Even more important, though, is that none of the currently available comprehension assessments is based in a viable or articulated theory of comprehension. And none can give us a detailed or convincing picture of how serious the problem of comprehension achievement in the United States is. These considerations, as well as the thinking about the nature of reading comprehension represented in this document, create a demand for new kinds of assessment strategies and instruments that (1) more robustly reflect the dynamic, developmental nature of comprehension; (2) represent adequately the interactions among the dimensions of reader, activity, text, and context; and (3) satisfy criteria set forth in psychometric theory.

Currently, widely used comprehension assessments are heavily focused on only a few tasks: reading for immediate recall, reading for the gist of the meaning, and reading to infer or disambiguate word meaning. Assessment procedures to evaluate learners' capacities to modify old or build new knowledge structures, to use information acquired while reading to solve a problem, to evaluate texts on particular criteria, or to become absorbed in reading and develop affective or aesthetic responses to text have occasionally been developed for particular research programs but have not influenced standard assessment practices. Because knowledge, application, and engagement are the crucial consequences of reading with comprehension, assessments that reflect all three are needed. Further, the absence of attention to these consequences in widely used reading assessments diminishes the emphasis on them in instructional practices as well.

What We Need in the Area of Comprehension Assessments

The entire research enterprise sketched out in this report depends on having a more adequate system of instrumentation for assessing reading comprehension. A satisfactory assessment system is a prerequisite to making progress with all aspects of the research agenda we propose. Thus we argue that investing in improved assessments has very high priority. It is clear that we cannot even sketch the seriousness of the problem of reading comprehension in the United States or the nature of the decline in comprehension outcomes that is the source of much worry until we have an assessment system that can be used across the developmental range of interest and that assesses the same construct across that range.

Assessing the effect of changes in instruction depends on having valid, reliable, and sensitive assessments. The effect of assessment on instruction is a question that constitutes a research agenda of its own, particularly in this highly accountability-oriented era of education reform. But the power of high-stakes assessments over instruction and curriculum can be somewhat mitigated if teachers have available alternative assessment options that give them more useful information.

Any system of reading assessments should reflect the full array of important reading comprehension consequences. We argue that a research program to establish expectable levels of performance for children of different ages and grades on this full array of consequences is necessary. Such a program is a prerequisite to developing performance criteria at different age and grade levels and to pursuing questions about reader differences associated with instructional histories, social class, language, and culture in reading comprehension outcomes.

Although the reading comprehension consequences defined above constitute the basis for designing a comprehension assessment that would reflect success, our view suggests that assessments designed to reflect readers' cognitive, motivational, and linguistic resources as they approach a reading activity are also necessary. For instance, when the outcomes assessment identifies children who are performing below par, process assessments could help indicate why their reading comprehension is poor. Further, diagnostic assessments are crucial in dissecting the effect of particular instructional or intervention practices. Ideally, we would move ultimately toward assessment systems that can also reflect the dynamic nature of comprehension, for example, by assessing increments of knowledge about vocabulary and particular target domains that result from interaction with particular texts.

We see the development of an assessment system for reading comprehension as having a very high priority. Such a system should be based in contemporary approaches to test development and evaluation. We recognize that developing a comprehensive, reliable, and valid assessment system is a long-term project. Crucial for such a system are the criteria for judging performance across the developmental span. Nonetheless, a substantial start could be made in the short run, either by targeting the assessment of outcomes and reader resources as a major task of the research agenda or by encouraging the development of prototype assessments for outcomes and reader resources within other research efforts (such as research focused on instructional efficacy). Such an effort is central to pursuing larger research agendas, such as longitudinal work to create a picture of the development of reading comprehension, a large-scale effort to determine how U.S. children are functioning as readers, or a systematic pursuit of differences in reading comprehension performance related to cultural background, social class, and language status.

The approach to assessment proposed here differs from current approaches to reading assessment in that it would both grow out of and contribute to the development of an appropriately rich and elaborated theory of reading comprehension. Assessment procedures generated by this approach are thus more likely to be influenced and changed by theoretically grounded reading research. Our approach also highly values the utility of assessment for instruction. Of course, comprehensive assessment systems can place high demands of time on students and teachers; thus, we have an obligation to develop assessments that are embedded in and supportive of instruction, rather than limited to serving the needs of researchers.

A comprehensive assessment program reflecting the thinking about reading comprehension presented here would have to satisfy many requirements that have not been addressed by any assessment instruments, while also satisfying the standard psychometric criteria. The minimum requirements for such a system follow:

- *Capacity to reflect authentic outcomes.* Although any particular assessment may not reflect the full array of consequences, the inclusion of a wider array than that currently being tested is crucial. For example, students' beliefs about reading and about themselves as readers may support or obstruct their optimal development as comprehenders; teachers may benefit enormously from having ways to elicit and assess such beliefs.

- *Congruence between assessments and the processes involved in comprehension.* Assessments that target particular operations involved in comprehension must be available, in the interest of revealing inter- and intra-individual differences that might inform our understanding of the comprehension process and of outcome differences. The dimensionality of the instruments in relation to theory should be clearly apparent.

- *Developmental sensitivity.* Any assessment system needs to be sensitive across the full developmental range of interest and to reflect developmentally central phenomena related to comprehension. Assessments of young children's reading tend to focus on word reading rather than on comprehension. Assessments of listening comprehension and of oral language production, both of which are highly related to reading comprehension, are rare and tend not to be included in reading assessment systems despite their clear relevance. The available listening comprehension assessments for young children do not reflect children's rich oral language–processing capacities, because they reflect neither the full complexity of their sentence processing nor the domain of discourse skills.

- *Capacity to identify individual children as poor comprehenders.* An effective assessment system should be able to identify individual children as poor comprehenders, not only in terms of prerequisite skills such as fluency in word identification and decoding, but also in terms of cognitive deficits and gaps in relevant knowledge (background, domain specific, etc.) that might adversely affect reading and comprehension, even in children who have adequate word-level skills. It is also critically important that such a system be able to identify early any child who is apt to encounter difficulties in reading comprehension because of limited resources to carry out one or another operation involved in comprehension.

- *Capacity to identify subtypes of poor comprehenders.* Reading comprehension is complexly determined. It therefore follows that comprehension difficulties could come about because of deficiencies in one or another of the components of comprehension specified in the model. Thus, an effective assessment system should be able to identify subtypes of poor comprehenders in terms of the components and desired outcomes of comprehension. It should also be capable of identifying both intra- and inter-individual differences in acquiring the knowledge and skills necessary for becoming a good comprehender.

- *Instructional sensitivity.* Two major purposes for assessments are to inform instruction and to reflect the effect of instruction or intervention. Thus, an effective assessment system should provide not only important information about a child's relative standing in appropriate normative populations (school, state, and national norms groups), but also important information about the child's relative strengths and weaknesses for purposes of educational planning.

- *Openness to intra-individual differences.* Understanding the performance of an individual often requires attending to differences in performance across activities with varying purposes and with a variety of texts and text types.

- *Usefulness for instructional decisionmaking.* Assessments can inform instructional practice if they are designed to identify domains that instruction might target, rather than to provide summary scores useful only for comparison with other learners' scores. Another aspect of utility for instructional decisionmaking is the transparency of the information provided by the test given to teachers without technical training.

- *Adaptability with respect to individual, social, linguistic, and cultural variation.* Good tests of reading comprehension, of listening comprehension, and of oral language production target authentic outcomes and reflect key component processes. If performance on a task reflects differences owing to individual, social, linguistic, or cultural variations that are not directly related to reading comprehension performance, the tests are inadequate for the purposes of the research agenda we propose here.

- *A basis in measurement theory and psychometrics.* This basis should address reliability within scales and over time, as well as multiple components of validity at the item level, concurrently with other measures and predictively relative to the longer-term development of reading proficiency. Studies of the dimensionality of the instruments in relationship to the theory underpinning their construction are particularly important. Test construction and evaluation of instruments are important areas of investigation and are highly relevant to our proposed research agenda.

Clearly, no single assessment would meet all these criteria. Instead, we propose an integrated system of assessments, some of which may be particularly appropriate for particular groups (e.g., emergent or beginning readers, older struggling readers, second-language readers, or readers with a particular interest in dinosaurs). Further, the various assessments included in the system would address different purposes, such as a portmanteau assessment for accountability or screening purposes, diagnostic assessments for guiding intervention, curriculum-linked assessments for guiding instruction, and so on. Given that we are proposing multiple assessments, we believe that studies of their dimensionality and of the interrelations of these dimensions across measures are especially critical.

A sample of issues that would certainly arise in the process of developing a comprehensive assessment system for reading comprehension follows:

- The effect of various response formats on performance.

- Variation in performance across types of text.

- The effect of nonprint information.

- The effect of various formats and accommodations on the test performance of learners of English as a second language.

- Variation in performance across a variety of types of discourse and genres, including hypertext.

- The effect on performance of specifying different purposes for reading.

- The capacity to differentiate domain-specific and reading-general operations.

- The need to reflect performance on literacy tasks typical of electronic reading, such as retrieval.

- The capacity to explore issues that go outside the traditional rubric of comprehension, such as scanning, intertextuality, domain-specific strategies, and consulting illustrations.

- The reliability, validity, and dimensionality of different assessment instruments and approaches.

Key Issues the Research Agenda Should Address

The key questions and issues that a research agenda on reading assessment needs to address and that are closely connected to the RRSG's proposed areas for future instruction research, include the following:

- How can the education community measure strategic, self-regulated reading, including a student's use of such strategies as questioning, comprehension monitoring, and organizing the knowledge gained from text?

- To what extent are performance-based assessments of reading sensitive to a student's competencies in such processes as vocabulary, cognitive strategies, writing ability, oral language (syntax), reading fluency, domain content knowledge of the texts, and such dispositions as motivation and self-efficacy for reading?

- How do we design valid and reliable measures of self-regulated, strategic reading that teachers can administer in the classroom to inform their instructional decisions?

- What informal assessments should teachers use to identify children who may need additional or modified instruction within the classroom to prevent a referral to special education services?

- How do we construct informal assessments to assist teachers in identifying how to help students who have low reading comprehension? For example, how could teachers identify which children need to be taught specific reading strategies or supported in domain knowledge acquisition or motivational development?

- What reading comprehension assessment could be both administered efficiently by all teachers in a school and used across grades to document student growth and guide teacher decisions about the appropriate texts, tasks, contexts, and learning activities for students?

- What available measures of motivation and engagement in reading can be linked to reading competencies, related to growth over time, and used to guide classroom learning activities?

- What measures of reading fluency can be used at the levels of the individual student, the classroom, and the school and can be related to reading comprehension and reading motivation?

- Which measures of reading comprehension are sensitive to specific forms of reading instruction and intervention for all readers?

- What are the dimensions evaluated by different assessments in relation to more traditional assessments and the proposed new approaches to assessment? How well does the dimensionality map onto the theories behind the development of the assessments?

Chapter Five

STRATEGIES FOR DEVELOPING A RESEARCH PROGRAM ON READING COMPREHENSION

Having a purposeful research agenda is only one prerequisite to developing a research program in any domain. In addition to formulating an array of desirable research activities, the education field will need to determine priorities—which aspects of the agenda to begin with and how to sequence the necessary research activities. Further, issues about the required infrastructure for the research effort must be addressed, as well as questions about how to sustain and steer the effort once it is under way so that knowledge can accumulate and its usability can be optimized. Considerations of the research methods are crucial, as are issues of funding levels and funding sources and collaboration among various potential funding agencies. We discuss these various issues in the following sections.

PREREQUISITES TO ESTABLISHING AN EXCELLENT EDUCATIONAL RESEARCH PROGRAM

This report makes clear that although the knowledge base in the area of reading comprehension encompasses a very large territory, it is extensive in some areas but limited in others. The RRSG has mapped the various domains of knowledge to help decisionmakers identify new research that will have the most effect on comprehension instruction and reading outcomes. In so doing, a number of prerequisites for the establishment of a successful and effective reading comprehension research program were identified. Those prerequisites include (1) establishing priorities, (2) building on strengths, (3) improving the status of education research, and (4) choosing methods appropriate to the task.

Establishing Priorities

The usability of knowledge now becomes the major criterion in establishing priorities—usability of knowledge in classrooms and in establishing policies. A research program should be judged not just on its methodological rigor, but also on its capacity to generate improvements in classroom practice, enhance curricula, enrich teacher preparation, and facilitate more-informative assessments.

1. *Criteria.* We suggest that an educational research effort that focuses only on reading comprehension as a field of research will be insufficient. The effort must also focus within reading comprehension on the highest-utility research topics. We have presented three domains of research within reading comprehension that we argue are of high priority—research on instruction, on teacher preparation, and on assessment. Even within those broad topics, further prioritizing is needed. Consulting with the research community will be key in developing likely priorities; at some point, though, decisive leadership will be needed.

Topics that are of high priority in the program of research on reading comprehension should be judged on the following criteria:

- How much knowledge has already been accumulated about the relevant aspects of comprehension?

- How significantly will expanding the knowledge base in the way proposed affect theory development?

- How important will exploring the instructional applications that might emerge from the research be to improving outcomes?

- To what extent will relevant applications enhance, extend, and expand current practice, rather than represent minor modifications to it?

2. *Tensions.* Any proposed research program represents a compromise between focus and breadth. Establishing priorities is not a formulaic procedure, but one that requires wisdom in weighing various criteria. It may be helpful to note a number of points that arose in our deliberations as we tried to establish priorities.

- *Tension between focusing on a specific age range versus a wider age range.* We discussed at some length the value of focusing our questions more specifically on a particular age range, for example, on kindergarten through grade 3, where most current reading reform efforts are targeted, or on the middle and high school grades, where practitioners are most concerned with effective reading comprehension instruction. We chose not to limit the age range of interest for a number of reasons. First, we did not wish to suggest that reading comprehension should be ignored in reading instruction in the primary grades; many accomplishments of kindergarten, grade 1, and grade 2 readers are directly relevant to current and future comprehension success, as are accomplishments in language even of preschool-age children. Second, in recognizing the practical challenges facing the content area teacher in middle and secondary school classes, and the degree to which those challenges are intricately related to reading comprehension, we did not wish to downplay the importance of research on this age range. Third, our conceptualization of reading comprehension is inherently developmental, encompassing precursors that develop in the preschool and primary school years as well as outcomes displayed in secondary school. This conception precludes restricting the age range of interest.

- *Tension between priorities derived from our analysis of research and practice and priorities determined by other factors.* We recognize that competing priorities exist within any research program. For example, priorities are derived from political realities, are associated with the availability of fiscal and human resources, are limited by the practicalities of certain kinds of research undertakings, and are related to the likelihood that results will actually be used to change practice. The group that produced this report limited itself to thinking about what the education community needs to know. Obviously, the ultimately selected research agenda will also need to incorporate the effects of other factors in selecting research targets.

- *Tension between research that is well embedded in existing knowledge and theory and research that is truly innovative.* Researchers want to generate novel conceptualizations and revolutionary findings. Practice is often better served by smaller increments to our knowledge, such as knowing whether a student's comprehension of a text read in English is enhanced or impeded by discussing the meaning in the student's first language or deciding whether vocabulary instruction should incorporate writing sentences with the new words. Since the utility of knowledge is a major criterion, we obviously endorse research efforts that will generate modest increments to the quality of practice. At the same time, research efforts laying down the basis for future improvements in practice in domains that are not yet close to practical utility should not be ignored.

- *Tension between immediate payoff and longer-term research efforts.* Although research priorities tend to be attached to questions or problems, planning a research effort requires thinking about a packet of activities that fit together and address practical as well as intellectual issues. Thus, we suggest that those conducting the research planning effort consider a strategy for soliciting short-term and long-term projects simultaneously. Short-term projects, such as evaluating well-founded instructional interventions, could generate useful outcomes relatively quickly. Long-term undertakings could be designed to underpin future improvements in practice by expanding the education community's basic understanding of reading comprehension. For example, a multisite, large-scale longitudinal study of reading comprehension development would be a long-term project. The entire research effort needs to be strategic and orchestrated. Although some of its components will have no immediate payoff, an understanding of how they might contribute ultimately to improving practice should always be required.

- *Tension between preplanned and emergent research priorities.* The RRSG achieved a remarkable degree of consensus on the formulation of issues in reading comprehension. It did not conclude, though, that its report should be an unfiltered basis for soliciting research proposals, in part because we agreed on the need to let the quality of research proposed partly determine the research priorities. Bad research on an extremely important topic is not likely to advance the field as much as excellent research on a slightly less pressing topic. Thus, we suggest that any solicitation of proposals be formulated with enough flexibility to allow the field to demonstrate what it can do well, while maintaining sufficient focus so that a coherent research program develops.

Building on Strengths

The quality of reading instruction in the primary grades in U.S. schools has benefited from the products of a 25-year program of research focused on understanding the development of word reading and on formulating interventions for children experiencing difficulties in word reading. We propose a focus on reading comprehension in part to build on these improvements in educational practice and in part to build a stronger research base for improving practice in preschool settings. It is clear that the benefits to reading outcomes that accrue from improved instruction in word reading will be limited if children do not also have access to improved instruction in vocabulary, oral language production, writing, text analysis, and other factors that contribute to comprehension. Such instruction is crucial even in the preschool years for children whose oral language skills are limited, and improved instruction needs to continue throughout the school years. Thus, the focus on reading comprehension we propose complements the currently funded research agenda on word reading, while benefiting from the advances the current research has made possible.

Improving the Status of Educational Research

Before an educational research program can demand support, it must address widespread doubts concerning the quality, relevance, and usefulness of its research. Therefore, educational funders should base their funding decisions not only on the intellectual credibility of a program but also on its practical utility. We suggest that the field of reading research take at least three steps to promote that effort.

1. *Ensure programmatic efforts.* High-utility research efforts are planned as long-term and cumulative undertakings. Changes in practice should not depend on the results of a single study or an attractive new idea; they should be based on well-replicated findings consistent with broader theoretical understandings. This presupposes a process to ensure that the research builds on previous findings and that the results of the various related research efforts are systematically accumulated, reviewed, and analyzed. These cumulative analyses should then become the subject of dissemination and the basis for changes in practice. Of course, the likelihood that research efforts will build on and inform one another is greatly enhanced if efforts are taken to build a collaborative community of researchers.

2. *Develop a community of researchers.* Research relevant to reading comprehension has been carried out within a variety of disciplines (linguistics, sociolinguistics, discourse processing, anthropology, psychology, and cognitive science) and by individuals working in quite distinct fields. In addition, the field of reading itself is sociologically somewhat complex, as emblematized by the existence of several organizations of reading researchers (International Reading Association, National Reading Conference, Society for the Scientific Study of Reading) with only partially overlapping membership and by strong constituencies of reading researchers within other organizations (American Educational Research Association, Society for Text and Discourse, Society for Research in Child Development). Making progress in reading comprehension research will require creating links across the now distinct subfields and subgroups. We suggest below that well-designed proposal review procedures can contribute substantially to forming a community of reading researchers linked by their common intellectual focus.

3. *Make both research- and practice-based knowledge optimally usable for all.* The challenge of improving reading comprehension is intrinsically a practical challenge, and reflective practitioners constitute a source of knowledge that is insufficiently represented in journals or in research proposals. If work on reading comprehension is to affect practice within our lifetimes, the concerns of practitioners need to be incorporated from the beginning. The work

must be seen as operating in Pasteur's quadrant[1] rather than as being exported to schools after the research papers are published. Mechanisms for distinguishing excellent from mediocre practice, for reviewing and accumulating the knowledge of effective practitioners, and for incorporating practitioner expertise into the research process need to be developed and nurtured.

METHODS APPROPRIATE TO THE TASK

The RRSG considered at length the issue of methodologies that are necessary to address the research questions identified by the committee. There was consensus among the members that a range of methodologies was not only necessary but also essential to ensuring rigorous responses to the various research questions. Further, the field of educational research possesses a diverse array of well-formulated, widely used methods for the conduct of rigorous research. Methods that have proven useful to advancing educational research include (1) experimental and quasi-experimental designs (Pedhazur & Schmelkin, 1991); (2) structural equation modeling (Nevitt & Hancock, 2000); (3) hierarchical linear modeling (Lee, 2000); (4) meta-analysis in experimental research (Schafer, 1999); (5) discourse analysis (Cazden, 1988); (6) video analysis (Stigler, Gallimore, & Hiebert, 2000); (7) classroom observational analysis (Turner & Meyer, 2000); and (8) verbal protocol analysis (Pressley & Afflerbach, 1995).

The body of knowledge about instruction in reading comprehension has been informed by a wide range of research methods. The power of this diversity is that converging evidence now exists for a substantial majority of the claims presented above regarding the principles of instructional practice. The principle that explicit strategy instruction increases comprehension is supported by two quite different forms of empirical studies. For example, the NRP (2000) summarized experiments showing the effects of instruction on the learning of strategies and on reading comprehension. To complement that evidence, case studies of teachers nominated as outstanding also report that these exemplary teachers provide explicit strategy instruction within the classroom context (Pressley et al., 2001). However, these examples do not imply that our knowledge is completely formed on this principle. For example, the conditions for the use of strategies are not fully explicated in either the experimental literature or the case study literature. However, this convergence does suggest that strategy

---

[1]Pasteur's quadrant refers to the quadrant of research defined by simultaneous contribution to basic and applied problems. Pasteur's contributions to the understanding of infection and contamination constituted theoretical breakthroughs at the same time that they also formed a basis for fighting disease and promoting public health.

instruction is a promising starting point for new research on reading comprehension instruction.

Statistical modeling has been advanced to permit the examination of critical aspects of complex problems such as reading comprehension instruction. For instance, structural equation modeling (SEM) allows investigators to study latent variables. Such variables represent the shared variance (e.g., the essential overlap in measurement) between two measured constructs. This is especially useful in reading comprehension research because valid and reliable measures of instructional variables, such as strategy instruction or autonomy support, are in the process of being developed. Further, SEM permits the study of mediation among classroom constructs, student characteristics, and student achievement outcomes. Hierarchical linear modeling (HLM) increases our capacity to study the effects of instruction on reading comprehension by permitting the investigator to eliminate variance in achievement attributable to unwanted sources (Lee, 2000). Especially with large data sets, or with quasi-experimental designs, variance in outcome variables that is not experimentally controlled can be statistically removed from the classroom instructional effects that are of theoretical importance. Both SEM and HLM permit investigators to form growth variables reflecting the slope and curvature of student improvement in reading comprehension or allied variables, such as reading motivation or content knowledge gained from reading.

To complement strong statistical modeling, in-depth analysis techniques permit investigators to examine the cognitive processes of readers through verbal protocol analysis (Pressley & Afflerbach, 1995). In this procedure, students think aloud while reading, and their verbal reports are examined for the qualities of their cognitive self-regulation and other higher-order thinking activities. As procedures for analyzing videotapes have advanced, widely shared guidelines for collecting, transcribing, interpreting, coding, and analyzing data have become available (Erickson, 1992; Stigler et al., 1999). These data are multivariate and interactionist. They can convey the complexity of classroom instruction. However, videotapes are necessarily limited to a few classrooms. When such data are linked to national (or state) probability samples, they can reveal generalizable patterns of instruction. Such patterns represent both the depth of classroom instruction and the breadth of generalization for the findings. Thus, methodological tools that are readily accessible to all investigators permit a diversity of approaches to research, as required in the multifaceted field of reading comprehension instruction.

Further, any substantial research effort will likely need to involve a combination of different approaches and different types of data requiring adherence to multiple evidentiary standards. In the interest of rigor, it is imperative that the methodology selected to address a research question be driven by the question itself and not by arbitrary judgments that some methods are stronger than others. For that matter, it is also not possible to make clear-cut divisions across types of methodologies, for a number of reasons:

- Classes of methodologies overlap to a large extent.

- There is no intrinsic ranking of values associated with any particular methodology.

- High levels of rigor can be defined for any form of disciplined inquiry, whether classified as qualitative or quantitative.

- Methodologies can be assessed only with reference to the research questions they are being used to answer.

Among quantitatively oriented studies, true experiments, of course, represent an ideal methodology for assessing the effect of instruction or intervention. True experiments are sometimes not feasible, though, since their successful implementation requires a set of conditions that cannot always be met in educational settings. In these cases, well-controlled quasi-experiments provide a standard of evidence that, although not as high as that of true experiments, is acceptable. Quantitative studies, including program evaluations, are typically enriched by the inclusion of methods that simultaneously provide descriptive and correlational data on, for example, the interaction of learner characteristics and response to intervention. Similarly, some methodologies that are qualitative and observational may have strong quantitative components, such as the observation and coding of classroom teaching behaviors in a time-by-activity framework essential to evaluating the effects of instructional strategies on student achievement.

Some questions call for ethnographic methods. For example, how do teachers and principals respond to the introduction of a new reading comprehension intervention into a school? Qualitative methods are often the most appropriate ones when the goal is discovery. For example, in-depth qualitative studies on bilingual students' use of metacognitive and cognitive strategies while reading in two languages have generated information on their reading that would have been otherwise difficult to obtain. Qualitative methods are also highly desirable when in-depth information is needed about important components of an intervention's functioning. Such information may illuminate, for example, whether the intervention is likely to be undermined or supported within a school. In addition, qualitative methods are useful for providing a cultural perspective on why certain groups respond the way they do to instruction, or for describing how teachers' practices differentially affect students' reading engagement and performance.

Thus, scientifically rigorous research studies use methods appropriate to the research questions of interest. In many instances, multiple methodologies blend descriptive, correlational, and experimental methods in the more quantitative area with a range of qualitative methods essential to addressing the questions of interest. It is also possible that the appropriate methodology of interest will be predominantly one or another type, although there is substantial variability in the characteristics of a single methodology that defies simply lumping methods into categories.

When multiple types of evidence can be cited in support of a particular conclusion, a greater capacity exists for building consensus, ensuring the translation of research to practice, and supporting the sustainability of research-based practices. We hope that one aspect of this research agenda will be to increase the receptivity of educational thinking to the value of rigorous research and to stimulate the active discussion of research methods and their appropriate application. A program of research, especially one structured across several years, is ideally characterized by procedures to guide selection of questions through a process of setting research priorities. Such a program also ensures that findings can be replicated, deepens understanding, charts progress, and assesses the degree of convergence across studies and research methods. The research program on reading comprehension that we propose here should be a model for effectively choosing and using appropriate and diverse methods.

THE RESEARCH INFRASTRUCTURE: ORGANIZING FOR PROGRAMMATIC RESEARCH ON READING COMPREHENSION

Procedures for getting from here to there also need to be in place. These procedures should at least encompass decisions about how Requests for Applications (RFAs) will be researched and written, who should serve on review panels, and how the accumulation of research findings will be monitored to serve as input to later RFAs.

To ensure that a long-term, large-scale initiative in reading comprehension research is successful, several infrastructure issues must be addressed. Concerns about the quality of educational research and the oversight of projects in the field are widespread. Efforts to extend these resources by collaborations across research entities have enhanced the educational research mission and reflect the judicious use of resources by all the agencies involved in these efforts. Such efforts should be extended, no matter what changes in the organizational structure for education research funding might be undertaken.

1. *Leadership and professionalism.* For this initiative to be successful, the RRSG recommends the following steps to ensure intellectual leadership and long-term planning:

- A director should be named to oversee this initiative and related reading research projects.

- The director should interact and collaborate with individuals across the various federal research entities involved with reading research.

- The director should interact with the field, help develop proposals, and help synthesize the knowledge base that will emanate from this and other federally sponsored reading research initiatives.

- The director should not be responsible for review.

As part of this implementation, criteria for evaluating research proposals and procedures for training reviewers and evaluating the quality of reviews need to be developed. A standing review panel with staggered, long-term appointments should be established. Panel members should have expertise that reflects the diversity of the research projects and the methodologies that this initiative is likely to attract. Creating this panel will help to establish continuity in review as well as to possibly provide an advisory component to the reading research program proposed here. This approach to review will provide considerable feedback to investigators in the field, thus contributing to enhanced research expertise. By virtue of the diversity of expertise on the panel, collaborations among researchers with different perspectives will be encouraged. Ultimately, such collaborations will lead to the integration of knowledge across subdisciplines that is essential to advancing our knowledge about reading and instruction. Individuals with limited independent research experience should not be placed on the panel. No reviewer should be appointed to this panel without training and a trial period on the panel, and procedures for terminating reviewers who fail to discharge their responsibilities should be established.

2. *Coordination.* There is an urgent need to coordinate across current efforts, while letting agencies build on their comparative advantages and develop their own ecological niches. Each federal agency involved in educational research works with its own set of priorities and constraints. The National Institutes of Health (NIH), for example, are well positioned to fund intervention trials, but not to fund curriculum development. The National Science Foundation (NSF) has funded Research on Learning Environments and other valuable demonstration projects, but these have so far had limited effect on schools or curricula. The OERI has historically funded a wide array of efforts, including basic research, demonstrations, training, development, technical assistance, and dissemination projects; the payoff from OERI's flexibility has been undermined, though, by its traditionally low funding levels and its failure to focus on particular research topics. At present, funding for R&D ac-

tivities devoted to reading comprehension is lacking among federal agencies that support education research.

3. *Sustainability.* A fleeting, intermittent, underfunded, or token approach to research on reading comprehension will be a wasted effort. This problem needs sustained attention, support, and funding that cut across administrations and political constituencies. In our view, the size and scope of the effort and the depth of the commitment must be on a scale equal to federal efforts to cure cancer or to develop a network of communications satellites. A number of specific steps will support sustainability.

   a. *Regular syntheses.* Procedures for accumulating, reviewing, and synthesizing knowledge developed through the funded research could be built into the funding effort. The review panel, or perhaps a panel of advisors to the entire research undertaking, might oversee these regular synthesis efforts.

   b. *Talent development.* Sustaining the effort also depends on developing a cadre of well-trained investigators. Much of what we know today about reading comprehension comes from work carried out at the Center for the Study of Reading, which received funding in the late 1970s to mid-1980s. Many researchers active in the field today received their training at this center. A new generation of comprehension researchers is needed, however. To develop a cadre of investigators capable of high-quality research, the RRSG specifically recommends designing research training fellowships and developmental grant programs for young investigators, modeled perhaps on NIH's clinical- and young-investigator postdoctoral awards programs. The optimal training environments for young investigators would give them access to senior researchers from a variety of disciplines and would integrate access to first-rate research training with opportunities to learn about schools and classrooms in an authentic way.

   c. *Coordinated solicitations.* Once a reading comprehension agenda is established, research should be solicited in a variety of formats, guided by the nature of the problems under investigation. Solicitations should reflect a long-term plan that incorporates a mix of short-term, medium-term, and long-term goals. The crafting of these solicitations should exhibit continuity, reflecting, for example, feedback on the success of earlier solicitations and the knowledge accumulated about the research agenda. The solicitations should reflect an attempt to coordinate across the efforts of various agencies and initiatives. Although field-initiated research should continue to receive support, it is critical that high-quality reading comprehension research be facilitated through carefully crafted initiatives that reflect the priorities identified in this report and the body of knowledge about reading comprehension that will emerge from this initiative. Different types of grants should be supported, including grants that support multiple connected projects around coherent central themes with collaborations among investigators that are of sufficient scale to address the complex issues involved in research on reading comprehension.

d. *Development work.* To sustain and extend the research effort, a systematic procedure for fostering the development of curricula, software, and instructional programs also needs to be in place. Often the practices that rest on research fail to receive prompt distribution because publishers have not yet rewritten their textbooks to reflect those practices or because the professional development efforts for bringing them to scale are inadequate. Attention to publishing, to software development, and to procedures for influencing teacher educational and professional development is needed from the beginning of the research planning.

e. *Sufficient funding.* The effort described in this report requires a significantly greater level of funding than is currently available for educational research. Improving reading comprehension outcomes in a systematic, research-based way will demand a substantial increase in basic knowledge about comprehension processes and large-scale efforts to implement and evaluate improved instructional, teacher preparation, and professional development programs. Urgent national priorities cannot be addressed without adequate resources. Significant federal funding has been appropriated to address such priorities as establishing satellite communications networks, fighting AIDS, curing cancer, and developing stealth bombers. Our view is that failures in reading comprehension are equally as urgent and equally as complicated; we cannot expect the educational equivalent of radar or the polio vaccine. Nor can we expect to make significant progress without a sum of money comparable to what is available for addressing other urgent national priorities. The U.S. government investment in R&D is between 2 and 3 percent of all national expenditures (gross domestic product). For example, in the areas of health, energy, and transportation, the United States invests between 2 and 3 percent of the budgeted dollars in R&D. In contrast, only 0.3 percent of the expenditures focused on K–12 education are spent on R&D (Office of Science and Technology, 1998). If, as a nation, we committed the same level of research-dollar funding to education research as we currently commit to other areas, reading comprehension outcomes could be substantially improved in the next 20 years.

This report on a proposed research agenda for reading comprehension, like the public draft of the report issued in 2000 that preceded it, is intended to serve as a foundation for a dialog between the U.S. Department of Education and other agencies that fund education R&D and researchers and practitioners in the field of the study of reading. By consulting with researchers and practitioners, these agencies can generate the broad base of information and political support that is essential to any federally funded education R&D effort.

The first draft of this report was commented on extensively during 2000 and 2001 through solicited reviews, feedback that was posted to the Achievement for All website (www.rand.org/multi/achievementforall), and questions and comments received during various conference presentations. Those many comments served to stimulate the RRSG's deep rethinking of key issues, which is reflected in this report.

Like any other document dealing with a topic as timely as research in education, this report is likely to become somewhat obsolete in the coming years. If the lines of research the RRSG proposes are pursued, new knowledge concerning reading comprehension may surface, the RRSG's proposed hypotheses on reading comprehension may be either strengthened or disproved, and the conclusions contained in this report may need to be revisited. Indeed, the conception of reading comprehension that has guided the RRSG's deliberations may need significant revision.

New knowledge and conceptions related to ways to improve all students' reading comprehension will inevitably emerge from a research program such as the one we propose. We recommend that funding agencies commission future study groups to assess and synthesize that knowledge and thereby point to new directions and priorities for research. The RRSG hopes that this report, in addition to providing guidance to current R&D programs, sets forth a useful base upon which those future study groups can build.

AN EXPANDED REVIEW OF THE RESEARCH ON VARIABILITY IN READING COMPREHENSION

This appendix contains an extended overview of the discussion in Chapter Three on variability in the three elements of reading comprehension—reader, text, and activity.

VARIABILITY IN READERS

In this section, we review research on the dimensions associated with variation in what readers bring to the activity of comprehending any particular text. We see variation among readers as being analyzable at four levels:

- *Sociocultural factors* help us understand differences among readers in the way they define comprehension, the nature of opportunities that readers have to learn to comprehend, and the texts and comprehension activities that they value. For example, learners from some social groups experience a lack of congruence between their own definitions of literacy and those they encounter at school, whereas those from other social groups find the school-based texts and literacy activities familiar.

- *Group membership* may have an effect on certain reader capabilities directly or on reader access to support for acquiring comprehension capabilities. For example, teachers may have varying expectations of literacy success for children from low- versus middle-income families. Second-language readers are likely in general to have less-extensive vocabulary knowledge than first-language readers, and recent immigrants are likely to be less familiar with presupposed background knowledge than long-term residents.

- *Individual differences* among readers go beyond those that correlate with sociocultural or group factors, reflecting the effect of biological, familial, or idiosyncratic factors. For example, the individual capacities that codetermine success in literacy acquisition, such as short-term memory, vocabulary knowledge, or sensitivity to discourse markers, can show large differences among children from the same social group or family.

- *Intra-individual differences* encompass the same dimensions as individual differences but arise from the fact that readers' deployment of their capabilities varies as a function of setting, text, and purpose for reading.

We review what we know and what we need to know about the many sources of reader variability in comprehension, noting explicitly that the correlations found between certain sociocultural and group factors on the one hand and individual or intra-individual differences on the other cannot be taken to indicate causal relations.

It will be evident from our review that considerably less is known about cultural and social sources of variability, or about the specifics of group sources, than about the reader differences related to inter- and intra-individual cognitive and motivational capacities. The reading processes of readers from backgrounds other than European-American have been investigated, sometimes from a sociocultural and sometimes from a group-differences perspective (see García, Pearson, & Jiménez, 1994; García, 2000, for reviews). Studying these groups helps us understand variability in reading comprehension because it extends the range on many relevant variables beyond that available within the European-American community and because the effect of other sources of variability may well differ as a function of group membership.

In each of the following subsections documenting various sources of reader variability, we consider first the research dealing with younger children, typically preschool and primary-grade children, then discuss older learners. Under inter- and intra-individual differences, though, we make the break slightly later, between preadolescent and adolescent readers, to accommodate the most frequent groupings in the literature.

Social-Cultural Influences

It is in some sense inappropriate to subordinate the discussion of social and cultural influences under reader variability, since in fact we are starting from an assumption that sociocultural influences infuse all reading and all learning. Nonetheless, it is clear that much research has conceptualized the challenge of universal high achievement as, in part, a problem of adapting schools to the degree of sociocultural diversity they now contain. Thus, we review in this section the research that attributes reader variability to sociocultural factors. As we will show in the next section, such group differences may significantly contribute to performance differences that may be observed in children from different backgrounds.

Preschool Through Primary-Grade Readers. Although all students have to learn how to adapt to school norms and mores (e.g., a student must raise his or her hand to be called on and ask permission to go to the bathroom), students who are not European-American and middle class are often at a disadvantage because they typically do not belong to their teacher's primary discourse community (see Cazden, 1988). Heath's research in the Piedmont region of the Carolinas showed that middle-class teachers expected their preschool children to respond to their literacy instruction in the same way that they expected their primary-grade students to respond (Heath, 1981, 1982). In contrast, children and parents from a working-class African-American community held beliefs about appropriate social interaction that conflicted with the teachers' beliefs. Because of such differences, the teachers viewed the African-American children as having deficits in their language and literacy abilities, for example, and were not able to engage them in effective literacy instruction. Valdés (1996) reported similar findings for immigrant Mexican children and their teachers. In their homes, the children were taught to respect others by not engaging in displays of knowledge, whereas the teachers expected the children to demonstrate what they knew. This discrepancy between home and school expectations often worked to the children's disadvantage because the teachers misperceived them as being less capable and placed them in lower reading groups.

Researchers (e.g., Juel, Griffith, & Gough, 1986) have compared the performance of African-American and Latino students with that of European-American students on a range of variables, such as word recognition, spelling, reading comprehension, and writing. Although the researchers took into account one or two sociocultural variables, such as ethnicity/race or socioeconomic status, they sometimes ignored other sociocultural variables, such as dialect or second-language status, that might have influenced their assessment of the students' performance or the interpretation of the data. For example, in a comparison of grades 1 and 2 European-American, African-American, and Latino students, Juel et al. reported that ethnicity and oral language strongly influenced the students' grade 1 year-end performance on phonemic awareness and to a lesser extent their grade 2 year-end performance. However, they did not take into account the variation in students' oral pronunciation of standard English that was due to dialect or second-language status.

Other researchers have focused on the reading performance and instruction of dialect speakers (e.g., Burke, Pflaum, & Knafle, 1982; Labov, 1982). They concluded that teachers' negative reactions to students' use of dialect adversely affected the type of instruction that the students received. Teachers' negative reactions were determined to have more of an effect on students' reading comprehension development than the students' use of dialect features.

These sociocultural factors produce readers who interact with text differently from the way European-American students do, since their preferred discourse forms may not appear in the most commonly used texts. They also receive access to a different set of reading activities because they are disproportionately placed in the lowest reading groups or lowest tracks where isolated-skill instruction dominates (e.g., Allington, 1983; Nystrand, 1990).

These examples clearly show that membership in different groups defined, in part, by factors that may appreciably affect proficiency in reading and reading comprehension per se—factors such as social class, ethnicity, and native language—can, indeed, have a significant effect on early reading development. Thus, research evaluating the relative contribution of such factors to early reading development as well as their interaction with other factors contributing to variability in such development (capacity differences) is an important area of inquiry in need of further study.

Preadolescent and Adolescent Readers. Social cultures offer a wealth of positions that readers can assume, and each position requires certain attributes. For example, to assume the position of "good reader," an individual must possess certain abilities that are verifiable and recognizable to others who occupy that same position (McDermott & Varenne, 1995). But how students end up inhabiting some positions and not others in their classroom environments is sometimes a matter of their being placed into those positions because of differential instruction, teacher attitudes, and certain expectations. Researchers working within a sociocultural framework recognize the possibility that youth who are routinely described in school as resistant readers may actually be readers who use alternative literacy practices, such as predicting the next episode in the Japanese animé Dragonball-Z (Alvermann, 2001) and using football statistics to structure an essay about the economic connections between athletes and commercial enterprises. A productive research focus would highlight situational contexts that promote reading comprehension both in and out of school for all adolescents.

Researchers who investigated older students' reading comprehension from a sociocultural perspective focused primarily on cultural schemata (e.g., Reynolds, Taylor, Steffensen, Shirey, & Anderson, 1982) as a source of variability. They reported that when students read culturally familiar material, they read it faster, recalled it more accurately, and made fewer comprehension errors. However, the researchers did not develop profiles of expert and novice readers from various backgrounds. As a result, no information is available on how students from these backgrounds resolved dialect or language problems or varied in their strategy use or motivation.

Group Differences

We include group differences as a focus of our interest, even though they are to some extent coterminous with sociocultural sources of variability, because a fairly large body of work has considered group membership (e.g., social class group, racial group, ethnic group, native language group) without relating the findings to cultural factors. Further, some identified groups (e.g., children growing up in poverty) or group-related factors (e.g., the more-limited English vocabulary associated with speakers of English as a second language) cannot be defined as cultural or culture-related, and some potentially influential factors (e.g., family income, attendance at good versus poor schools) are likely to be correlated with group membership. We are not concluding that membership in any of these groups can itself cause particular comprehension outcomes; rather, we are suggesting that documenting the differences may generate hypotheses about causal connections.

Preschool and Primary Readers. In research conducted with young children, Sonnenschein and colleagues (Sonnenschein, Baker, Serpell, Scher, Truitt, & Munsterman, 1997) found that children from lower-income brackets had fewer opportunities to interact with print and play with words than did children from higher-income brackets. Similarly, Whitehurst and Lonigan (1998) reported that children from low-income homes had less experience with books, writing, rhymes, and other literacy-promoting activities than did children from higher-income homes. In contrast, children from higher-income homes tended to enter kindergarten with more of such experience, as evidenced in greater alphabetic knowledge, greater ability to generate invented spellings, greater knowledge of print concepts, and so forth. Thus, in general, children from low-income families are less well prepared to engage in formal literacy learning than are those from higher-income families. However, as Goldenberg (2001) points out: "Family socioeconomic effects on achievement are in fact quite modest; and . . . effective school programs will help more children achieve, regardless of their economic class" (p. 216).

Another example of a group membership factor that significantly affects early literacy development is second-language learning. Tabors and Snow (2001) recently reviewed research on language and literacy development in second-language learners from birth to age 8. They generally concluded that second-language learning differentially affects literacy development depending on such factors as the age at which second-language learning is initiated, the language in which exposure to print and early literacy instruction is initiated, the child's degree of proficiency in a first or second language, the child's proficiency in the language in which print exposure and literacy instruction begins, and the degree of support for first- and second-language learning and literacy development in both the home and school environments (see also Snow et al., 1998).

For example, whereas learning to read a second language is impeded by a child's limited proficiency in that language, learning to read the native language may facilitate a child's ability to learn to read a second language. Similarly, disruption of first-language learning by virtue of total immersion in second-language learning may impede language and literacy development in both. Thus, variability in both language and literacy development is greatly affected by the second-language learner's home and school environments.

Preadolescent and Adolescent Readers. Two indicators of the reading performance and academic engagement of older students (grades 4–12) in U.S. schools are data from NAEP, often termed "the nation's report card," and data on the dropout rate. Ever since NAEP has kept statistics on the reading performance of various groups, national samples of African-American, Latino, and Native-American students have scored significantly lower than national samples of European-American students. In 1992, 1994, and 1998, high percentages of African-American, Latino, and Native-American students scored below the basic level, or the lowest achievement level, for grades 4, 8, and 12 (Campbell, Hombo, & Mazzeo, 2000). The performance of English language learners is difficult to ascertain because NAEP has not differentiated these students' scores from the national sample unless they have been in U.S. schools for less than two years and their teachers have judged them incapable of participating in the assessment because of their limited English proficiency. Students who fit in the latter category are required to participate in NAEP but with accommodations. Not surprisingly, their NAEP reading performance is significantly lower than that of their European-American counterparts and, on average, is below the basic level. According to the National Center for Education Statistics, dropout rates for African-American, Latino, and Native-American students are considerably higher than those of European-American students. Clearly, if we want to improve the literacy performance of all students, we must pay more attention to the literacy instruction and performance of those groups of students who have historically been poorly served by U.S. schools.

More research has focused on the reading processes of older English language learners (grades 3–7) than on younger children (García, 2000). English language learners, when compared with monolingual English speakers, typically have less background knowledge relevant to topics in English texts or tests, know less English vocabulary, and have some difficulty with questions that rely on background knowledge (e.g., García, 1991). Researchers who explored how English language learners were making sense of reading in both of their languages reported that it was important to differentiate students who were successful English readers from those who were less successful (e.g., Jiménez, García, & Pearson, 1996). The successful English readers had a unitary view of reading and used strategies and knowledge that they had acquired in one language to approach reading in the other language. They also used bilingual strategies, such as cognates, paraphrased translating, code-mixing, and code-switching. The less-successful English readers did not use cross-linguistic transfer strategies and thought that they had to keep their two languages separate or they would become confused.

For younger children, various reading activities are differentially available. English language learners, regardless of the program in which they were enrolled, tended to receive passive, teacher-directed instruction of the sort that does not promote higher-order thinking or language development (Padrón, 1994; Ramirez, Yuen, & Ramey, 1991). Metacognitive and cognitive strategy instruction, such as reciprocal teaching and question-answer relationships, has shown promise with both English language learners and monolingual English speakers (see, e.g., Muniz-Swicegood, 1994).

We reiterate that when discussing group differences associated with race, second-language learning, and similar factors, research that emphasizes literacy processes at the level of the individual is not very illuminating unless we situate the individual's experience within the larger sociocultural and historical context (Buenning & Tollefson, 1987). Yet, the trend within literacy research has been to focus on the structural and formal properties of literacy, often seeing it as a technical problem that can be investigated without taking into account power relations and social practices (Wiley, 1996). When ethnic/racial and linguistic minorities are included in large-scale research, they often are part of a random sample, and specific information related to their actual literacy performance and improvement is not included in the data interpretation (García et al., 1994). At other times, projects have excluded these populations (Willis & Harris, 2000), erroneously generalizing to them the findings based on the experiences and instruction of European-American, middle-class, monolingual students. Given the discrepancy in literacy performance between the default monolingual European-American reader and readers from other ethnic/racial and linguistic groups, research efforts that specifically examine the literacy processes, performance, and engagement of students from diverse ethnic/racial and linguistic groups, and that take into account the larger sociocultural and historical contexts, are warranted.

Inter-Individual Differences

Describing and attempting to explain inter-individual differences in reading outcomes have been by far the most common undertakings of reading researchers. Indeed, many of the advances in our understanding of early reading development have emerged from studies that took an individual differences perspective. A systematic analysis of individual differences in the capabilities that relate to comprehension is a potential source of considerable insight about the process of comprehension.

Preschool and Elementary School Readers. Individual children vary in their reading comprehension abilities. Some of this variability, no doubt, reflects the procedures used to assess reading comprehension. However, variability in reader characteristics may also partially account for these differences. Thus, the differential development of a variety of capabilities and dispositions supporting reading comprehension may lead to patterns of relative strengths and weaknesses that are directly related to variations in reading comprehension abilities. Moreover, we have reason to believe that the relative contributions that different learner characteristics make to variability in reading comprehension ability change significantly during the course of reading development. For example, we know from research done over the past two decades that accurate and fluent (automatic) word recognition is a prerequisite for adequate reading comprehension and that language comprehension processes and higher-level processes affecting language comprehension (applying world knowledge, reasoning, etc.) do not become fully operative in comprehending text until the child has acquired such facility (Adams, 1990; Gough & Tunmer, 1986; Hoover & Gough, 1990; Perfetti, 1985; Stanovich, 1991; Sticht & James, 1984; Vellutino et al., 1991, 1994).

We also know that in learning to read in an orthography derived from an alphabet, the acquisition of facility in word recognition depends heavily on the acquisition of print concepts (printed words comprise letters, letters carry sound values, print proceeds from left to right, etc.), mastery of the alphabetic code, and oral language development, among other things, and that both word identification and alphabetic coding depend heavily on such phonological skills as phoneme awareness, name retrieval, and verbal memory. In fact, abundant evidence now shows that most children who have difficulty learning to read have deficient phoneme awareness and alphabetic coding skills and that such deficiencies are causally related to deficiencies in word recognition, spelling, and writing (Adams, 1990; Liberman, 1983; Snow et al., 1998; Vellutino, 1979, 1987).

There is also some reason to believe that deficiencies in vocabulary and oral language development can lead to deficiencies in the acquisition of word recognition and related phonological skills, especially in bilingual children and children from low-income families (Goldenberg, 2001; Dickinson & DeTemple, 1998; Snow, 1993; Snow, Barnes, Chandler, Goodman, & Hemphill, 1991; Strickland, 2001; Tabors & Snow, 2001; Vernon-Feagans, Hammer, Miccio, & Manlove, 2001; Whitehurst & Lonigan, 2001). However, recent observational and intervention studies have demonstrated that many such children are the victims of inadequate instruction, limitations in early literacy experience, or both (see, e.g., Blachman, 1997; Dickinson & DeTemple, 1998; Dickinson & Sprague, 2001; Neuman, 1999; Neuman & Roskos, 1990, 1997; Roskos & Neuman, 2001; Snow et al., 1991; Torgesen, Wagner, & Rashotte, 1999; Vellutino et al., 1996).

At the same time, substantial evidence indicates that the reading problems of a very small percentage of beginning readers are due, in significant measure, to basic deficits in phonological skills not accounted for by limited experience or poor instruction (Torgesen et al., 1999; Torgesen, 2000; Vellutino et al., 1996). Finally, we know that phonological skills deficits can occur even in children who are intellectually capable and who are not generally impaired in learning. In fact, a great deal of convergent evidence now indicates that measured intelligence is not highly or reliably correlated with basic reading subskills, such as word identification and letter-sound decoding, although it is often found to be significantly and reliably correlated with measures of reading comprehension (Fletcher, Shaywitz, Shankweiler, Katz, Liberman, Steubing, Francis, Fowler, & Shaywitz, 1994; Siegel, 1988; Stanovich & Siegel, 1994; Vellutino, Scanlon, & Lyon, 2000). Thus, reader differences in the acquisition of word-level skills are the primary source of variability in reading comprehension in beginning and elementary school–age readers. And because long-standing reading difficulties inevitably lead to deficiencies in higher-level language skills and knowledge sources that depend heavily on proficient reading (Stanovich, 1986; Vellutino, Scanlon, & Tanzman, 1988; Vellutino, Scanlon, & Spearing, 1995), the importance of fluency in word recognition to reading comprehension cannot be underestimated.

However, we also know that fluent word recognition is a necessary but not sufficient condition for successful reading comprehension and that other variables that directly or indirectly influence language comprehension are also critically important determinants of variability in reading comprehension. These variables include (1) vocabulary and linguistic knowledge, including oral language skills and an awareness of language structures; (2) nonlinguistic abilities and processes (attention, visualization, inferencing, reasoning, critical analysis, working memory, etc.); (3) engagement and motivation; (4) an understanding of the purposes and goals of reading; (5) discourse knowledge; (6) domain knowledge; and (7) cognitive and metacognitive strategy development. The degree to which these components develop in an individual child or adult may well account, in part, for individual differences in the development of reading comprehension abilities. Thus, such variables may also be usefully targeted in research evaluating inter-individual differences in reading comprehension.

For example, evidence from research conducted with both children and adults indicates that individual differences in language comprehension and related skills, such as vocabulary knowledge and syntactic competence, account for more of the variance in reading comprehension than do individual differences in word-level skills (i.e., word recognition and letter-sound decoding) in readers who have acquired enough facility in word recognition to comprehend in print what they would normally comprehend in spoken language (Bradley & Bryant, 1983; Curtis, 1980; Davis, 1944, 1968, 1972; Hoover & Gough, 1990; Neuman & Dickinson, 2001; Stanovitch, 1991; Sticht & James, 1984, Vellutino et al., 1991, 1994). There is also some evidence that individual differences in the awareness of linguistic structure (phonological awareness, syntactic awareness, pragmatic awareness, etc.) have an appreciable effect not only on the acquisition of word recognition skills but also on language and reading comprehension skills, especially in terms of the role that such awareness plays in comprehension monitoring (Tunmer, Herriman, & Nesdale, 1988). Thus, it is not surprising to find that individual differences in vocabulary knowledge, syntactic competence, and metalinguistic awareness, associated with neurodevelopmental and home background factors, are good predictors of literacy development and reading comprehension (Dickinson & DeTemple, 1998; Snow, 1993; Snow et al. 1991; Scarborough, 2001; Vellutino & Scanlon, 2001; Whitehurst & Lonigan, 2001). Moreover, deficiencies in one or more of these skills have been found to distinguish between good and poor comprehenders (Tunmer et al., 1988; Vellutino et al., 1991, 1994, 1996; Vellutino & Scanlon, 2001).

Similarly, the consistent finding across a broad age span that measures of intelligence tend to be strongly correlated with measures of language and reading comprehension (see Vellutino et al., 2000, for a recent review) provides strong evidence that intellectual skills such as reasoning, critical analysis, and inferencing ability are important sources of individual differences in reading comprehension, Thus, it is not surprising to find that measures of intelligence tend to distinguish between children who are skilled and less-skilled comprehenders, despite the fact that such measures do not reliably distinguish between children who are more- or less-skilled in word recognition and related phonological skills (Vellutino et al., 1996, 2000).

In the same vein, abundant evidence is available to show that individual differences in working memory are highly correlated with individual differences in language and reading comprehension (Baddeley, 1986; Baddeley & Logie, 1999; Cantor, Engle, & Hamilton, 1991; Daneman & Carpenter, 1980; Engle, Cantor, & Carullo, 1992; Engle, Tuholski, Laughlin, & Conway, 1999; Ericsson & Kintsch, 1995; Just & Carpenter, 1992). And although most of this work has been done with adults, some work has recently been done with children (see Swanson & Siegel, in press, and Vellutino, in press, for a review of this work). In general, the evidence suggests that individuals with a low working-memory capacity process language less effectively and are less effective comprehenders than individuals with high working-memory spans. The research with children is seminal, however, especially in terms of its implications for instruction, and more work needs to be done in this area.

A closely related area of inquiry is the study of individual differences in controlled and focused attention as it relates to skill in reading. Some researchers suggest that individual differences in maintaining controlled and focused attention are the primary source of individual differences in working-memory spans and, therefore, of individual differences in reading comprehension (Cantor et al., 1991; Engle et al., 1992, 1999; Swanson & Siegel, in press). However, this assumption is arguable (Ericsson & Kintsch, 1995; Vellutino, in press). That deficiencies in maintaining controlled and focused attention would have a deleterious effect on reading comprehension (and on the acquisition of skill in reading in general) seems a reasonable and valid assumption on its face, however. Some evidence supports this assumption (Shaywitz, Fletcher, & Shaywitz, 1995), but the relative contribution of attention deficits to deficiencies in reading comprehension remains to be further explored.

Another cognitive ability that might be an important source of individual differences in reading comprehension is the ability to visualize, especially as it relates to the use of illustrations and pictorial material as an aid to comprehension. Gyselinck and Tardieu (1999) reviewed the evidence for this relationship and generally concluded that a positive and reasonably strong correlation exists between the use of pictorial aids and comprehension. They point out, however, that individuals may differ in their ability to profit from such aids and suggest that the ability to visualize may be one source of such individual differences. The use of visual imagery as an aid to verbal memory has been extensively studied in both adults and children (e.g., Begg & Clark, 1975; Begg, Upfold, & Wilton, 1978; Paivio, 1971, 1986; Paivio & Begg, 1971; Pressley, 1977; Pressley & Miller, 1987; Vellutino & Scanlon, 1985; Vellutino et al., 1995). However, the research concerned with individual differences in visual-spatial ability as a determinant of variability in reading and language comprehension is seminal (e.g., see Reichle, Carpenter & Just, 2000; Hegarty, Carpenter, & Just, 1991; Mayer & Sims, 1994), and this also seems to be a useful area of inquiry.

Research documenting that a knowledge of linguistic discourse is an important source of individual differences in reading comprehension has a long history (Just & Carpenter, 1987; Mandler & Johnson, 1977; Stein & Glenn, 1979; Stein & Trabasso, 1981; van Oostendorp & Goldman, 1999), but most of this research has studied reading comprehension processes in adult skilled readers. Considerable research has focused on children's understanding of narrative text (Mandler & Johnson, 1977; Stein & Glenn, 1979; Stein & Trabasso, 1981), and some, but much less, work has studied children's understanding of expository text (Armbruster & Anderson, 1984; Taylor, 1985; see Graves & Slater, 1996, for a review). The available evidence suggests, however, that good comprehenders better appreciate discourse structure than do poor comprehenders, and they more effectively use such knowledge than do poor comprehenders.

Using cognitive and metacognitive strategies as an aid to reading comprehension also has a long history, and some research evidence indicates that good comprehenders are inclined to use such strategies more often and more effectively than poor comprehenders (e.g., Palincsar & Brown, 1984; Pearson & Fielding, 1991; Pressley, 2000; Tierney & Cunningham, 1984). This research also suggests that such strategies can be effectively taught and that their use will improve reading comprehension. In addition, there is some reason to believe that intervention that fosters the use of strategies—such as comprehension monitoring, use of linguistic context, and other meaning-based devices—to aid understanding (e.g., pictorial clues) will facilitate the acquisition of word recognition and phonological decoding skills as well as reading comprehension skills (Pinnell, Lyons, DeFord, & Bryk, 1994; Tunmer et al., 1988; Vellutino & Scanlon, in press). Thus, it seems that the role that cognitive and metacognitive strategies play in accounting for individual differences in acquiring both word-level and comprehension skills is worth additional study.

That engaged and intrinsically motivated children will become more proficient readers than less engaged and less intrinsically motivated children is a truism that generalizes across advantaged and disadvantaged populations and is supported by abundant evidence (e.g., Guthrie, Cox, Anderson, Harris, Mazzoni, & Rach, 1998; Guthrie, Van Meter, et al., 1998; Guthrie, Wigfield, & VonSecker, 2000; Snow et al., 1991; Strickland, 2001; Sweet, Guthrie, & Ng, 1998).

Motivated and engaged readers are also purposeful and goal-directed readers. The same research supports the generalization that purposeful and goal-directed readers become better comprehenders than less purposeful and less goal directed readers. Moreover, engaged, motivated, purposeful, and goal-directed readers also acquire more knowledge than those who are less engaged, less motivated, less purposeful, and less goal directed. Some of the most impressive research supporting this generalization comes from studies comparing individuals having high and low degrees of domain knowledge in given areas (knowledge of baseball, football, soccer, etc.). These groups were compared on measures evaluating comprehension of texts describing events in their area of expertise as well as on measures evaluating memory for factual information presented in these texts, while varying such relevant factors as verbal ability, reading ability, and IQ (e.g., Schneider, Koerkel, & Weinert, 1989; Recht & Leslie, 1988; Walker, 1987; Yekovich, Walker, Ogle, & Thompson, 1990). The common finding among these studies is that individuals having a high degree of knowledge in a given domain performed at a higher level on these measures than individuals having a low degree of knowledge in that domain, regardless of their aptitude in the other areas assessed. Such findings also underscore and support the important role played by individual differences in acquired knowledge—both world knowledge and domain knowledge—in accounting for variability in reading comprehension.

However, much more remains to be learned about the relationship between and among these different capabilities and dispositions on the one hand and the acquisition of skill in reading on the other. For example, a child's motivation to engage beginning reading as an academic enterprise and his or her success in doing do seem to be related to the child's initial preparedness for reading in terms of home background and emergent literacy skills, as well as to reading-related cognitive capabilities that set constraints on success in beginning reading. Similarly, a child's motivation to engage beginning reading and to sustain efforts in the interest of becoming a proficient reader seems to be related, in no small way, to the quality of reading instruction to which the child is exposed during both the beginning and the advanced stages of reading development. Obviously, instruction that capitalizes on the child's inherent interest and surrounds him or her with high-interest and readable materials (i.e., materials at the child's level of proficiency) appears to be more effective than instruction that does less; evidence supports this assertion (e.g., Hiebert & Martin, 2001; Morrow & Gambrell, 2001). Thus, research evaluating the relative contributions made by individual capabilities and dispositions to variability in reading comprehension at different phases of reading development is greatly needed.

Adolescent Readers. As with younger children, the differences in adolescent readers' motivation to read and their engagement with subject matter texts, broadly defined—for example, social studies textbooks, geologic maps, Internet sites, videos, magazines, and photographs—depends on a number of factors. Chief among these is the adolescent's perception of how competent he or she is as a reader. In adolescence, as in earlier and later life, it is the belief in the self (or the lack of such belief) that makes a difference in how competent the individual feels (Pajares, 1996). Providing adolescents who are experiencing reading difficulties with clear goals for a comprehension task and then giving feedback on the progress they are making can lead to increased self-efficacy and a greater use of comprehension strategies (Dillon, 1989; Schunk & Rice, 1993). As well, creating technology environments that heighten students' motivation to become independent readers and writers can increase their sense of competency (Kamil, Intrator, & Kim, 2000). The research is less clear, however, on the shifts that occur in students' motivation to read over time. Although decreases in intrinsic reading motivation have been noted as children move from the elementary grades to middle school, explanations vary about the cause, with a number of researchers attributing the decline to differences in instructional practices (Eccles, Wigfield, & Schiefele, 1998; Oldfather & McLaughlin, 1993).

A second determining factor in how adolescents respond differently to different subject matter texts lies in their ability to comprehend information that is new or that conflicts with their prior knowledge. Not all adolescents enter their middle and high school years with effective strategies for comprehending large chunks of text over relatively short periods of time. Nor do they possess adequate background knowledge and technical vocabularies for comprehending their assignments, although the importance of vocabulary knowledge to subject matter comprehension has been recognized since the 1920s (Whipple, 1925).

Research on vocabulary knowledge is best interpreted conditionally. It seems likely, for example, that for readers with reasonably well-developed background knowledge who are reading text with a large number of unfamiliar words, knowledge of words per se may be the most significant problem. If these same readers read a text with only a few unknown words, their ability to make inferences about word meanings might be a more important factor than their word knowledge. If, however, this same text involved culturally unfamiliar material or a topic of little interest to the reader, comprehension might again be difficult. We therefore believe that research is called for that examines how the relationship between vocabulary knowledge and reading comprehension depends on specific conditions, including the type of reader, type of text, proportion of unfamiliar words, their role in the text, and the purpose for reading or the outcome being considered. Because the relationship between word knowledge and conceptual knowledge is more variable among second-language readers, it is especially important to examine the contributions and interactions of these two types of knowledge for such readers.

Adolescents who fall behind in their course work are typically described as being "at-risk" of dropping out of school or, more recently, as "struggling readers" (Moore, Alvermann, & Hinchman, 2000). The struggling reader label is a contested term and one that means different things to different people. It sometimes refers to youth with clinically diagnosed reading disabilities as well as to those who are English language learners, underachieving, unmotivated, disenchanted, or generally unsuccessful in school literacy tasks that involve print-based texts. As such, these labels tell very little about the reader, although they do suggest ways of thinking about culture and adolescents who, for whatever reason, are thought to be achieving below their full potential as readers.

The research on struggling readers covers a broad spectrum and varies in specificity according to the perceived reasons for the struggle. For example, reviews of research that take into account individuals with clinically diagnosed reading disabilities (Shaywitz, Pugh, Jenner, Fulbright, Fletcher, Gore, & Shaywitz, 2000) focus on the cognitive basis for the struggle. Reviews of second-language reading, in contrast, encompass a much wider view of the reasons behind the struggle. In fact, the difficulties that English language learners experience are often spread over a vast array of sociocultural, motivational, and linguistic factors that vary with the population being studied (Bernhardt, 2000). These same factors are often manifested in the difficulties that monolingual adolescents experience when a reading problem is present. In their critique of culture as a disabling agent, McDermott and Varenne (1995) argue that society (for the problem does not lie solely with schools) *makes* struggling readers out of some adolescents who for any number of reasons have turned their backs on a version of literacy called school literacy.

A third factor contributing to inter-individual differences among adolescent readers has to do with their access to (and ability to use) new information communication technologies. The Internet figures prominently in the lives of American youth, particularly suburban youth (Barton, Hamilton, & Ivanic, 2000; Beach & Lundell, 1998). According to a phone survey of 754 teenagers and 754 of their parents reported by the Pew Internet and American Life Project in conjunction with a weeklong online discussion-group study conducted by the research firm Greenfield Online (Lenhart, Rainie, & Lewis, 2001), 17 million youths between the ages of 12 and 17 use the Internet. This number represents 73 percent of the young people in that age bracket. Moreover, close to 13 million adolescents use instant messaging (with one-quarter of that number saying that they pretend to be different people when online).

That literacy is reinventing itself through new digital technologies (Luke & Elkins, 1998; Moje, Young, Readence, & Moore, 2000) has enormous implications for how we view inter-individual differences among adolescents at the middle and high school levels (de Castell, 1996). Researchers working within a qualitative paradigm have found patterns in their data to suggest that adolescents who appear most at risk of failure in the academic literacy arena are sometimes the most adept at (and interested in) understanding how media texts work—in particular, how meaning gets produced and consumed. For example, O'Brien (1998, 2001) found in a four-year study of working-class adolescents deemed at risk of dropping out of high school that students were quite successful in producing their own electronic texts, such as multimedia documentaries, and critiquing media violence by using multiple forms of visual texts. Working alongside the students and their teachers in what came to be called the Literacy Lab, O'Brien observed that by not privileging print over other forms of literacy, the students appeared capable and literate. This finding is similar to one that Alvermann and her colleagues (Alvermann, Hagood, Heron, Hughes, Williams, & Jun, 2000) reported for their after-school study of 30 adolescents who participated in a 15-week Media Club project. Although the participants had scored in the lowest quartile on a standardized reading achievement test, they capably demonstrated their critical awareness of how a variety of popular media texts represented people, ideas, and events. They also engaged in literacy practices of their own choosing (what they called their "freedom activities"), which included searching the Internet for song lyrics, producing hair and fashion magazines, e-mailing knowledgeable others to obtain information on favorite rap groups, and so on. Activities such as these, along with numerous other examples in *Intermediality: The Teachers' Handbook of Critical Media Literacy* (Semali & Pailliotet, 1999), point to young people's interest in working with diverse symbol systems and their ability to be critical consumers, as well as producers, of multiple forms of text.

When multimedia texts offer text with visual and verbal information, the extant research on multimedia processing offers some guidelines for how information can be presented more effectively. According to a dual code theory of information processing (Paivio, 1986), visual information and verbal information are processed in separate codes. Thus, multimedia information that is processed both verbally and visually is hypothesized to be more memorable because there are two memory traces instead of one. In fact, some empirical research supports a dual coding hypothesis with multimedia information (Mayer, 1997; Mayer & Moreno, 1998; Plass, Chun, Mayer, & Leutner, 1998).

How prior knowledge influences learning with multimedia information is an important variable that has significant implications for evaluating and selecting appropriate texts for children. Balcytiene (1999) found that low-prior-knowledge students benefit from hypermedia more than high-prior-knowledge students in his research with college students' improvement in recognition task scores. Correspondingly, in a review of six studies with multimedia instruction, Mayer (1997) also found that learners with low prior knowledge performed better with multimedia. In contrast, Lawless and Kulikowich (1996) found that students who did not have enough relevant domain knowledge had difficulties with hypertext comprehension; they also found significant relationships among domain knowledge, strategy knowledge, and measures of recall.

Given the conflicting findings, it appears that the interaction of prior knowledge and subsequent learning from hypertext is also influenced by other task and learner variables. In a study with grade 2 children, Shin, Schallert, and Savenye (1994) found a significant interaction with learner control and the degree of prior knowledge the learner had, suggesting that low-prior-knowledge students would be more successful within a more limited learner-control environment.

This preliminary study holds important ramifications for the selection of multimedia documents for children, suggesting that children who have low subject matter expertise should have multimedia text with fewer user-controlled options for hypertext navigation and browsing. It also points out the importance of having a developmental perspective when considering the influence of dimensions of individual differences. Collectively, these studies underscore the importance of considering the learner's domain knowledge when selecting multimedia documents for a particular student. For example, in comparing multimedia with traditional text, Kozma (1991) notes how the transient nature of multimedia information versus the stability of regular text could pose more of a problem for novice and low-domain-knowledge students.

With respect to the special case of reading texts with hyperlinks, students may need additional strategies for proficient reading and navigation. Hypertexts, or electronic texts that include links to additional information or content, demand special skills for monitoring comprehension—the timing and navigation of links to prevent problems such as disorientation or distraction. In addition, children who are accustomed to reading linear documents may become confused or distracted by following links incorporated within the text of documents. Preliminary research has identified the potential role of strategy use in accounting for differential reading outcomes. The use of specific strategies— such as being able to identify important text nodes and read them longer (Gillingham, Garner, Guthrie, & Sawyer, 1989), being a self-regulated reader (Balcytiene, 1999), and using a variety of learning strategies (Davidson-Shivers, Rasmussen, & Bratton-Jeffery, 1997)—helped students' performance on various tasks.

Intra-Individual Differences

The topic of intra-individual differences has been somewhat underemphasized in research on reading, although practitioners are well aware of the degree to which a child's apparent reading proficiency can be influenced by the nature of the text being read or the activity being engaged in. We explore variability within readers in part because this topic offers insights for designing instruction.

Preschool, Primary, and Elementary Grades. Students differ from one another in how diverse their reading competencies and interests are. For example, some students read stories frequently and are expert in story comprehension, whereas they rarely read electronic text and are not highly competent with computers. However, other students may be competent with computer and Internet reading, whereas they are not proficient in interpreting written stories. These intra-individual differences are not well represented on current measures of reading comprehension and are seldom used productively in instruction. Moreover, intra-individual variability in the acquisition of reading competencies can be observed during each phase of reading development and is sometimes manifested in the uneven development of important skills and subskills that underlie proficient reading.

To illustrate, during the beginning phases of reading development, when children are acquiring basic word recognition, phonological (letter-sound) decoding, and text-processing skills, it is not uncommon to find significant imbalance in the acquisition of one or another of these skills in a given child, to the detriment of that child's progress in becoming a proficient, independent, and motivated reader (Vellutino et al., 1995; Vellutino & Scanlon, in press). This type of imbalance is, in most cases, a by-product of such important influences as home literacy experiences, the child's instructional program, or the particular way the child conceptualizes reading. Thus, one child may have a strong and growing sight word vocabulary and strong text-processing skills (comprehension monitoring, use of context, knowledge of story grammar, etc.), but little or no ability to use phonological decoding skills to help identify unfamiliar words encountered in text. Another child may have strong phonological decoding skills but a limited sight vocabulary and weak text-processing skills; as a result, this child is destined to become a letter-by-letter, word-by-word reader with a limited ability to comprehend what he or she reads. And still another child may have a strong sight vocabulary and strong phonological decoding skills but weak text-processing skills, as manifested in a limited sense of story structure; a limited sense of the pragmatic relations embedded in the text; little or no tendency to monitor understanding; and little or no use of semantic, syntactic, or pictorial clues to aid word identification and text comprehension. Such a child is also destined to become a word-by-word reader with little ability to comprehend what he or she reads. Thus, despite strengths in one or another aspect of reading, a child with weaknesses in one or more of the aforementioned reading subskills will have difficulty becoming a fluent and proficient reader. The goal of the practitioner must, therefore, be to assess and correct such weaknesses, while capitalizing on the child's strengths to facilitate growth in reading.

Of course, intra-individual differences in capabilities other than word recognition and rudimentary text-processing skills may also set limits on the child's growth in reading. They may also affect appreciably the child's ability to acquire knowledge in areas that depend, to some extent, on reading. For example, despite having adequately developed word recognition and phonological decoding skills, the child with limited vocabulary knowledge or limited world knowledge will have difficulty comprehending texts that presuppose such knowledge. Similarly, given the important role played by extensive and diverse reading in acquiring vocabulary knowledge, in encountering and representing the more abstract and more complex syntactic structures, and in acquiring a broad-based knowledge of discourse structure (Olson, 1977, 1994; Watson & Olson, 1987; Watson, 2001), the child who does little independent reading, and who is not motivated to read extensively and diversely, will be ill equipped to engage and profit from the broad array of expository and technical texts encountered in school learning, even if he or she has no basic intellectual deficits or basic deficits in reading or oral language development. Further, the child who has not acquired the cognitive and metacognitive strategies and study skills necessary to use reading as an instrument of learning will undoubtedly profit less from reading in a given domain than the child who has acquired these skills, along with the disposition and tenacity to use them, even if the two children have comparable reading and oral language skills (Palincsar & Brown, 1984; Pearson & Fielding, 1991; Pressley, 2000; Tierney & Cunningham, 1984). The child who is not motivated to acquire knowledge in a given domain or to engage the school curriculum and school learning at large, will not acquire much knowledge in any given domain and will not profit much from school learning in general.

These influences, either separately or in some combination, may be partly responsible for Venezky's (1998) finding, in a recent analysis of Slavin's Success for All intervention program (Slavin, Madden, Karweit, Dolan, & Wasik, 1992), that the reading comprehension scores of disadvantaged children who were graduates of this program were substantially below national normative standards, despite the fact that their scores on measures of word-level skills (word recognition, letter-sound decoding) were comparable to national standards. They may also be responsible, to some extent, for the well-known fourth-grade slump so often observed in the educational community, although alternative explanations, such as inadequacy of vocabulary knowledge, have also been proposed (Meichenbaum & Biemiller, 1998).

On the positive side, the tenacious and inquisitive child with basically strong intellectual skills, a high degree of intrinsic motivation to become a good student, strong study skills, and a positive and goal-directed attitude toward reading and school learning may acquire a level of proficiency in reading and writing that will allow him or her to become a good student, despite inherent limitations in reading-related linguistic abilities that make it difficult for that child to acquire the full range of literacy skills. Similarly, the child with a high degree of interest in gaining knowledge and expertise in a given domain (e.g., sports, wildlife, theater, computers) may acquire through reading and other vehicles a higher degree of knowledge and expertise in that domain than the child who has little interest in the domain, even if the former child has less intellectual, oral language, or reading ability than the latter child (Schneider et al., 1989; Recht & Leslie, 1988; Walker, 1987; Yekovich et al., 1990). Conversely, the child who has wide ranging and diverse interests, but little motivation and tenaciousness for acquiring a high degree of expertise in a given domain, is likely to acquire a substantial amount of world knowledge and perhaps a large number of facts (the proverbial "master of trivia"), but is unlikely to become an expert performer in any given domain.

Finally, the child who has strong capabilities and dispositions in most or all of the areas that contribute to variability in reading comprehension has the potential to become a proficient reader and successful achiever, provided that other important factors influencing achievement are favorable.

The challenge for researchers and practitioners alike is to acquire the means for assessing these intra-individual differences—that is, patterns of strengths and weaknesses—of the child. They must also develop instructional techniques and formats to help the child correct or compensate for weaknesses or limited interests in given domains, while using strengths and high-interest domains as the springboard for acquiring proficiency in reading and becoming an engaged, motivated, and successful student in the later grades.

Adolescent Readers. All the various issues we raised about the sources of inter-individual variability in adolescent readers could be recapitulated under the heading of intra-individual differences. Thus, domains of particular interest associated with varying degrees of engagement can lead adolescent readers to perform with much greater comprehension when reading about some topics than others. Further, patterns of strength or weakness in the domains of word-reading accuracy, fluency, comprehension strategies, vocabulary, domain knowledge, and so on can lead to performances that vary as a function of the characteristics of the text and of the task being engaged in. Little research directly addresses the issue of intra-individual differences in the adolescent reader; this clearly is a topic that needs more attention.

VARIABILITY IN TEXT

Understanding variability in the text dimension requires paying attention to several components and levels of the text being read and to what it affords to the reader trying to construct a representation of that text. The processes of reading and post-reading presumably have some connections to elements and features of the text. Vocabulary and syntax have traditionally been recognized as text attributes that have a strong effect on comprehension. However, researchers in discourse have identified text features that are linked to the content, mental models, pragmatic communication, discourse structure, and genre of the text. All of these levels are construed from the perspective of the sociocultural context of the readers and participants in the learning environment. Further, it is important to realize that particular features of the text create difficulty for particular readers engaged in particular activities; texts are not difficult or easy in and of themselves, but they become difficult or easy at the interface with readers and the purpose of the activity (see Figure 2.1 in Chapter Two).

Language and discourse researchers have identified the following general levels of text representation (Graesser, Millis, & Zwaan, 1997; Kintsch, 1998): the surface code (vocabulary and syntax), the propositional text base (explicit meaning of the content), the mental model (deeper referential content), pragmatic communication, and discourse structure and genre. The *surface code* consists of the exact wording and syntax of the sentences. The *propositional text base* contains explicit propositions in the text (i.e., statements, idea units) in a stripped-down form that preserves the meaning, but not the verbatim surface code. The *mental model* (or what is sometimes called the situation model) is the referential microworld of what the text is about; it contains the people, setting, states, actions, and events that are either explicitly mentioned or inferentially suggested by the text. The *pragmatic communication* level refers to the exchange between the speech participants, between the reader and the writer, or between the narrator and the audience. Sometimes this level is not manifested directly in the text, but at other times it is explicit (e.g., "The purpose of this article is to persuade you to . . ." or "This manual will show you how to assemble your bookshelves"). *Discourse structure and genre* are the rhetorical structure of the discourse as well as the category of discourse, such as narration, exposition, persuasion, and so on. Each level is discussed below.

Surface Code: Vocabulary

The vocabulary load of a text has repeatedly been demonstrated to be a powerful predictor of the comprehensibility of the text (Freebody & Anderson, 1983). Readability research has consistently identified two factors, one representing vocabulary load or difficulty and one representing syntactic complexity, with the first having the greater loading (Klare, 1974–75, 1976). The data linking vocabulary and text difficulty are predominantly correlational, and readability formulas have been rightly criticized as being inadequate either as causal explanations of text difficult or as guidelines for text revision (e.g., Davison & Kantor, 1982). Nevertheless, as we discuss elsewhere in this report, under some circumstances, vocabulary per se can be a source of comprehension difficulty.

Surface Code: Syntax

Sentences are segmented into phrases that are structurally related systematically. The effect of syntax on sentence processing has a long history in psycholinguistics (Fodor, Bever, & Garrett, 1974; Mitchell, 1994). Sentences with complex syntax may present comprehension problems or a high load on working memory. This occurs when a sentence is embedded, dense, ambiguous, or ungrammatical. Some of the problematic syntactic constructions are highlighted below.

1. *Left-embedded syntax instead of right-branching syntax.* Sentences with left-embedded syntax occur when many clauses, prepositional phrases, and qualifiers are encountered before the main verb of the main clause: "The processing of left-branching utterances which are characterized, for exam-

ple, by relative clauses modifying the subject can, especially for young or unpracticed readers, pose great difficulty." Such sentences are difficult because the respondent needs to hold a large amount of partially interpreted code in memory before he or she receives the main proposition.

2. *Dense clauses.* Sentences with a syntactically dense clause pack too many higher-level constituents or idea units (i.e., propositions) within a single clause. Readers need to have a high analytical ability to unpack the various idea units. An example is the following question on a U.S. Census questionnaire: "Approximately how many miles was it one way to the place you hunted small game most often in this state?" It may facilitate comprehension to break up the single clause into multiple independent clauses. A dense clause, sentence, or question has a high ratio of propositions or higher-level syntactic constituents per word. Oral language has a simpler syntax than printed text (Chafe & Tannen, 1987), typically with only one new idea per intonation unit (roughly a clause). In contrast, the language of print packs many new idea units into a clause and thereby overloads working memory. Thus, it can simplify comprehension challenges if writers write the way they talk.

3. *Dense noun-phrases.* A dense noun-phrase has too many adjectives and adverbs modifying the head noun: "The regular monthly or quarterly mortgage payment."

4. *Structural ambiguity.* Ambiguous syntactic structures occur when two or more syntactic structures can be assigned to a sentence. For example, the following question from a U.S. Census survey is structurally ambiguous in a number of ways: "Is this house or apartment owned by you or someone in this household with a mortgage or loan?"

5. *Garden path sentences.* In "garden path" sentences, the respondent starts out assigning one syntactic structure to a sentence, but eventually realizes that the structure is wrong and has to reinterpret the syntactic structure. The following is an example of a garden path question: "Did you know the owner of the apartment sold the property?" This garden path question can be disambiguated with the word *that* to signal the existence of a complement clause: "Did you know that the owner of the apartment sold the property?"

6. *Complex Boolean expressions.* These sentences have a high density of logical operators: *or, and, not,* or *if-then.* Disjunctions (expressions with *or*) quickly impose a load on working memory because the respondent needs to keep track of different options and possibilities. The following question illustrates this: "At the time of the incident, were you covered by any medical insurance, or were you eligible for benefits from any other type of health benefits program, such as Medicaid, Veterans Administration, or Public Welfare?"

Propositional Text Base

The text base captures the meaning of the explicit propositions and includes the necessary bridging inferences that the respondent needs to connect the explicit propositions (van Dijk & Kintsch, 1983; Kintsch, 1998). The text base is a propositional code that preserves the arguments (nouns, pronouns, embedded propositions) and the predicates (main verbs, adjectives, connectives), but not the more subtle details about verb tense and aspect and about deictic references (*here, there, now, then, this, that*). Examples of propositions follow: The cam is between the cylinder and the spring [*between* (cam, cylinder, spring)]; the singer repaired the computer [repair (singer, computer)]; and if the cam rotates, the spring contracts [*if* (rotate [cam]), (contract [spring])]. The most common method of scoring text-recall protocols is to segment the text into proposition units and to score the proportion of these units that are recalled correctly.

Mental Model

The mental model (or situation model) is a deeper conceptual depiction of what the text is about (Graesser et al., 1997; Johnson-Laird, 1983; Mayer, 1992; van Oostendorp & Goldman, 1999). Researchers have analyzed the contents of the mental models in expository texts in great detail. Some of the common types of referential content follow:

- *Class inclusion.* One concept is a subtype or subclass of another concept. For example, a Pentium is a computer (is a device).

- *Spatial layout.* Spatial relations exist among regions and entities in regions. For example, a pin is in a cylinder (is in a lock). A spring surrounds a rod.

- *Compositional structure.* Components have subparts and subcomponents. For example, a computer has (as parts) a monitor, a keyboard, a central processing unit, and memory.

- *Procedures and plans.* A sequence of steps or actions in a procedure accomplishes a goal. An example would be the steps in removing the hard drive in a computer.

- *Causal chains and networks.* An event is caused by a sequence of events and enabling states. An example is the sequence of events that lead to a polluted lake.

- *Agents.* These are organized sets, such as people, organizations, countries, and complex software units. Examples are organizational charts and client-server networks.

- *Others.* These include property descriptions, quantitative specifications, and rules.

We note, once again, that some aspects of the mental model are directly captured by elements and features in the text, whereas other aspects are inferred by the reader during comprehension.

A mental model may also include a more formal representation of the problem (Nathan, Kintsch, & Young, 1992), a level that takes into account the formal (mathematical) relations that exist between the elements described in the statement of a problem. In addition to everyday general world knowledge, there needs to be scientific and mathematical knowledge on the relations between the variables in the problem. Thus, a student may create an appropriate mental model of the entities and events in the text, but still be incapable of translating this into scientific concepts and principles.

Regarding coherence *between* levels, there needs to be a mapping between the elements of the representation at one level and the elements at another level. For example, the surface code has words and syntactic patterns that signal content features at the level of the situation model. Comprehension suffers when the surface code and the mental model clash. If the text stated that "the key is turned after the cylinder rotates," there would be a discrepancy between the order of events in the situation model (the key is turned *before* the cylinder rotates) and the surface code (clause X *after* clause Y).

Pragmatic Communication

The communication level captures the pragmatic context that frames the messages in the text (Beck, McKeown, Hamilton, & Kucan, 1997; Graesser, Bowers, Olde, & Pomeroy, 1999; Nystrand, 1986; Rosenblatt, 1978/1994; Schraw & Bruning, 1996). Simply put, who is communicating to whom? What author is talking to what reader? Is there a narrator communicating to an addressee? For example, the text about a dishwasher would be composed quite differently for readers trying to repair a dishwasher, those trying to assemble a new dishwasher, and for those deciding which dishwasher to purchase. A good technical writer anticipates whether the reader will be a repairman, an assembler, or a potential customer. The writer crafts the texts for these different purposes, and these differences are reflected in the textual features.

Discourse Structure and Genre

Discourse analysts have proposed several classification schemes, called genres, that are organized in a multilevel hierarchical taxonomy or in a multidimensional space (Biber, 1988). Some examples of text genres at a basic level of classification are science textbooks, literary novels, repair manuals, comic books, and science fiction novels. The traditional general categories are narration, exposition, persuasion, and description (Brooks & Warren, 1972).We can imagine a detailed fine-grained typology of text genre. A rich literature on the composition and comprehension of narrative texts includes research on story grammars (Mandler, 1984) and on the construction of the point/moral/themes of stories (Williams, 1993). We currently have very little understanding about students' awareness of discourse genre for expository texts. Meyer & Freedle (1984) and Chambliss (in press) have investigated the rhetorical composition of several subclasses of expository texts, such as problem+solution, claim+evidence, compare-contrast, definition+example, and so on.

Discourse structure is the rhetorical organization of a text that coherently connects text elements and constituents and that relates the content to the messages of the author. Discourse structure includes text genre, the distinction between given (old) and new information in the discourse context, the points (main messages) that the author intends to convey, the topic structure, the pragmatic goals or plans of the communicative exchange, and the function of the speech acts (e.g., assertion, question, directive, evaluation). Discourse knowledge builds on linguistic knowledge but is distinct from it.

VARIABILITY IN ACTIVITY

In this section, the three types of variability in the reading comprehension activity—variability in purpose, variability in operations, and variability in consequences—are examined in depth.

Purpose

When most adults read, the purpose organizing the activity is the reader's purpose. In instructional activities, there are imposed purposes that may or may not penetrate to the consciousness of the learner. Indeed, some teacher-imposed purposes may conflict with the purposes that some children, in particular those from certain social and cultural groups, bring to the reading activity. Further, teacher-imposed purposes may be relatively limited (read this text to answer this question) or more dynamic (read this text to learn something novel from it) or even long term (read this text to apply and practice a newly learned strategy). Teachers can also construct authentic purposes for reading that students enthusiastically adopt, such as reading for writing (Horowitz, in press), reading for presentation (Schank, 1999; Bransford, Goldman, & Vye, 1991; Bransford, Brown, & Cocking, 1999), and reading to support long-distance communication (Leu, 1994). Various teacher-defined purposes relate to the organization of instructional contexts for reading.

Although this is not an exhaustive list, the dimensions of variability in instructional contexts that may be relevant for the activity of reading include the following:

- *Unit focus.* Instruction that focuses on reading individual words or brief sentences obviously provides less scope for comprehension instruction than activities that take longer texts as the unit of relevance.

- *Teacher-defined task.* During comprehension instruction, teachers may define the task for the student as one of recovering specific information (read this passage and then answer detailed questions), one of constructing the main idea, one of analyzing, and so on. These various imposed purposes create varying opportunities to learn from the specific text and to learn about comprehending texts more broadly.

- *Teacher goals, expectations and epistemological beliefs.* It is well known from studies of grouping that teachers define different goals for different groups of students. When the varying goals come from assessment-based data about students' greatest instructional needs, of course they are highly appropriate. When they are based on depressed expectations about the capacities of groups of children, however, they can generate instruction in which very simple purposes for reading are defined, such as finding particular words or answering low-level questions.

- *Curriculum.* Curricula define to a large extent the reading purposes, by virtue of structuring activities for teachers.

- *Grouping.* Purposeful and flexible grouping, such as that used in Success for All (Slavin et al., 1992), creates different short- and long-term purposes for readers in different groups. Such grouping strategies work well if the instruction indeed becomes more efficient so that all readers move into the higher-level groups where more challenging purposes can be formulated.

- *Pacing.* Setting the pace for reading instruction is an important ingredient in priming students for success in reading. To some extent, pacing depends on the fluency of individual students. Striking a balance between keeping students challenged by teaching advanced reading skills and ensuring that all students have the appropriate level of fluency to handle the demands of new lessons is a routine part of skillful teaching.

- *Coverage.* Especially when teaching reading in the content areas, teachers should carefully plan how much material to cover on a particular topic. Factors they should consider when making judgments about the scope of coverage include concept complexity, specialized vocabulary, and the depth of understanding they expect students to achieve. They should teach comprehension strategies that foster deep understanding of relevant content matter and give students ample opportunities to employ them.

- *Setting.* Common differences between the purposes of electronic and paper texts emerge. Much reading on the Internet, for example, involves scanning in search of specific sorts of information. It would be inefficient to use the same deep comprehension strategies during that phase of electronic text reading as during the reading of an assigned content area text.

Of course, these dimensions of variability in purpose and related organizational factors are in themselves determined by other factors, many of which are known to relate to reading comprehension outcomes as well. For example, we know that reading instruction in schools serving poor children is likely to be more exclusively skill focused and to incorporate less focus on text interpretation (Allington & McGill-Franzen, 1989; Nystrand, 1990). Schools serving poor children are much less likely to have lengthy texts widely available in classrooms, and instruction in such schools is more likely to require students to read and write single words and brief texts than longer units (Duke, 2000). High-stakes assessments that are limited to low-level competencies, low-inference items, and forced-choice questions may influence teachers to de-emphasize higher levels of comprehension in their instruction. Some schools and school systems have extremely rich electronic environments for reading activities, whereas others either have no computers available or have computers but only low-level practice-oriented software.

Comprehension instruction varies with the age and the reading level of the learner. Children just starting to learn the alphabetic principle benefit from activities that elicit and model the comprehension of texts read aloud (Beck & McKeown, 2001), whereas for more advanced readers, instruction in strategies for comprehending texts they themselves read can be helpful (NRP, 2000). Instruction focused on capacities related to comprehension, such as vocabulary and oral language production, is also rare in preschool and primary grades and is largely ineffective in the later grades (Meichenbaum & Biemiller, 1998; Morrison, Jacobs, & Swinyard, 1999; Stahl & Fairbanks, 1986). Many have argued that explicit attention to oral language development and vocabulary in the preschool and primary grades constitutes a crucial aspect of comprehension instruction (Whitehurst & Lonigan, 2001); although we know that older readers also benefit from aural exposure to rich text (Stahl, Richek, & Vandevier, 1991), it is unclear whether there are advantages to aural versus literate exposure for children who themselves can read the text.

These dimensions of variability can to some extent be seen as the product of higher-level factors influencing the organization of schools and of instruction, such as the following:

- *Age of child.* Reading instruction for primary school children tends to focus on word-reading skills. As children get older, those who have mastered word reading may well enter instructional contexts where a greater focus on comprehension instruction is possible, but all do not have access to such contexts.

- *Stakes.* The nature of the accountability system in place, and of the specific assessment instruments used, can affect contexts for instruction by narrowing or broadening the curriculum and by directing instructional attention to particular purposes, consequences, and response formats.

- *Information about children.* Teachers vary enormously in the degree to which they have access to and make sensible use of information about children's reading abilities. Such differences can influence how much they can individualize instruction to address particular children's areas of strength and weakness.

- *Demographics.* Lower-level and more exclusively skill-focused instruction is more likely to take place in schools serving low-income children (Allington, 1983; Nystrand, 1990). Further, English language learners, regardless of the type of program in which they are enrolled, tend to receive passive, teacher-directed instruction of the type that does not promote higher-order thinking or language development (Padrón, 1994; Ramirez et al., 1991).

- *Environment.* The environments in U.S. classrooms vary enormously in the availability of resources that might promote comprehension activities. Aspects of those environmental differences that might particularly influence comprehension include the availability of a wide variety of texts, access to electronic media, and the availability of intervention for children who fail to make adequate progress.

- *Curriculum.* Although the curriculum in some schools is under the control of the teacher, in others it is largely dictated by the principal or the superintendent. Reading curricula, but also mathematics, science, and social studies curricula, provide varying levels of opportunity for teachers to engage in instruction that promotes comprehension and the acquisition of comprehension skills.

Operations

The operations engaged in during reading activity consist of cognitive processes and procedures that extract information from the text and construct meaningful representations. These processes reflect the constraints of the text, the context, and the reader. Some of these operations become automatic through extensive learning and practice, so they consume very few attentional resources and little consciousness. For example, the operations of written-word decoding, lexical access, and syntactic parsing become automatic in proficient readers. Other operations are more deliberate processes that demand attention and consciousness, such as constructing a mental model and generating some classes of inference. This section identifies operations during reading that are needed for comprehension to be successful.

Attention. As with any cognitive task, adequate reading comprehension implies sufficient ability to attend to and concentrate on material being read in a controlled and focused manner. Research in the study of attentional processes has made it clear that information pickup in any knowledge domain is virtually impossible if attentional processes are fractionated and inefficiently deployed, although we do not fully understand the means by which an individual filters irrelevant from relevant information (e.g., Broadbent, 1958; Posner & Snyder, 1975; Norman & Bobrow, 1975; Gernsbacher, 1997). However, we do know something about some of the factors that may affect the ability to read for meaning in an efficient and focused manner. As we indicated earlier, attention to the meaning of a text is compromised by a lack of fluency in word identification because of the inefficient deployment of cognitive resources occasioned by word identification problems (LaBerge & Samuels, 1974; Perfetti, 1985). Similarly, the difficulty level or the structural characteristics of the text (e.g., Graesser & Bertus, 1998; Hiebert & Martin, 2001) are other factors that may compromise a reader's ability to attend to the meaning of a text. The reader's ability to negotiate these text features may be appreciably affected by such variables as his or her level of oral language development (e.g., Dickinson & Snow, 1987; Snow et al., 1991), background knowledge (Kintsch, 1998; van Oostendorp & Goldman, 1999), familiarity with text genre (Lorch & van den Broek, 1997), and interest in the content of the text (Alexander & Murphy, 1998; Morrow & Gambrell, 2001), in addition to his or her fluency in word identification. Finally, the ability to attend to and pick up information from a text may be appreciably affected by inherent differences in the ability to deploy attentional resources in a controlled and focused manner (Barkley, 1990). Thus, it is clear that how attentional processes affect reading comprehension is a multidimensional question in need of further study.

Written Word Decoding. Adequate facility in reading comprehension implies adequate facility in decoding written words. Readers who have difficulties in acquiring word-decoding skills will have trouble progressing to the deeper levels of language analysis; therefore, their comprehension will suffer (Perfetti, 1994; Stanovich, 1986). Readers with a slow or an inadequate mastery of word decoding may attempt to compensate by relying on meaning and context to drive comprehension, but at the cost of glossing over important details in the text. When readers read at the normal rate of 250 to 400 words per minute, a large amount of the reading time variance is explained by features of the surface code (Carver, 1992; Haberlandt & Graesser, 1985; Perfetti, 1994), such as the number of letters, the number of syllables, and the word frequency. These features are less predictive of reading time when the students study the text for a longer time.

Fluency. Fluent reading is the performance of a complex skill. Fluent reading is reading that is fast and accurate. It reflects the ability to decode without effort, to read aloud smoothly with expression that indicates the text's prosodic features (i.e., appropriate pacing and phrasing), and to comprehend easily what is read. A fluent reader achieves comprehension without consciousness or awareness of the many component tasks involved. With practice, low-level word recognition becomes automatic, which reduces the need for allocating attention to visual coding processes during reading and allows more attentional resources to be allocated to comprehension (LaBerge & Samuels, 1974; Perfetti, 1985). As readers become fluent, they also gradually begin to recognize the syntactic structures or segments in printed text and thereby compensate for its lack of prosodic information (punctuation does provide some assistance; Schreiber, 1987).

The complex set of processes that underlie fluency can be broken down in several ways (Meyer & Felton, 1999), for example, in the lower-level processes of phonological or orthographic processing (Breznitz, in press); in making connections between semantic and phonological processes (Wolf, Bowers, & Biddle, 2000); and in syntactic processing, which may be observable in oral language at early ages (Schreiber, 1980).

There is evidence that fluency is an index of comprehension, although the evidence is only correlational. Oral reading fluency (ORF) measures fluency simply as the number of words read aloud correctly per minute (Fuchs, Fuchs, Hosp, & Jenkins, 2001). There is a substantial correlation between ORF and standardized reading comprehension performance. This correlation is sometimes higher than the correlation between the standardized test and other direct measures of reading comprehension (Fuchs et al., 2001). These findings are based on samples of both learning-disabled and non-learning-disabled students at varying reading levels, who were assessed with a variety of criterion measures of reading comprehension and whose oral reading fluency was assessed on both instructional-level texts and fixed-level texts, (e.g., Jenkins, Fuchs, Espin, van den

Broek, & Deno, 2000; Levy, Abello, & Lysynchuk, 1997; Torgesen, Rashotte, & Alexander, in press).

Many informal procedures have been devised to assess fluency, although no standardized tests of reading fluency exist. Miscue analysis and running records have been used. Informal reading inventories assess the reading of grade-level passages both aloud and silently. Although most measures evaluate both speed and accuracy, NAEP (Pinnell, Pikulski, Wixson, Campbell, Gough, & Beatty, 1995) added a measure of pausing efficiency, which assessed sensitivity to prosodic cues.

Syntactic Parsing. Parsing is the process of segmenting words into constituents, assigning the constituents to syntactic categories, and interrelating the constituents structurally. The effect of syntax on sentence processing has a long history in psycholinguistics (Fodor et al., 1974; Mitchell, 1994). Sentences with complex syntax may present comprehension problems or a high load on working memory when a sentence is left-embedded, dense, ambiguous, garden-path, ungrammatical, or replete with logical expressions (*or, and, not,* or *if-then*), as we discussed earlier in this appendix.

The fields of psycholinguistics and discourse psychology have investigated how syntactically complex constructions influence reading time, working memory load, and comprehension (Fodor et al., 1974; Mitchell, 1994; Carpenter, Miyake, & Just, 1994). Unfortunately, much of the psycholinguistics work has focused on sentences in isolation, out of a discourse context, so it is unclear how problematic these constructions are when students read naturalistic print. We do know that the syntax is comparatively complex in expository text (Chafe & Tannen, 1987) and that syntactic complexity has a robust effect on elderly readers of expository text (Kemper, Jackson, Cheung, & Anagnopoulos, 1993), so the obvious prediction is that syntactic complexity will be a robust predictor of reading performance when expository text is read in virtually all subject populations. A more detailed analysis of syntactic processing in children is needed.

Readability indexes normally include word frequency and number of words in the sentence in the formulas, but not specific aspects of syntactic processing. The tests of syntax that are available present sentences in isolation, not in a discourse context. One direction for future research is to investigate the role of syntax in the comprehension of expository text in different subject populations, with a research team that includes experts in linguistics, psycholinguistics, discourse psychology, discourse processing, psychometrics, and education. The training of students on syntax will require computer technologies and improved teaching methods.

Constructing the Propositional Text Base. The reader segments the text into proposition units, interrelates the propositions structurally, and builds the necessary bridging inferences that are needed to connect the explicit propositions (van Dijk & Kintsch, 1983; Kintsch, 1998). The text base is retained in memory for hours, much longer than the surface code is (Kintsch, 1998). Empirical evidence suggests that a measurable amount of time is needed to construct the propositional text base. Reading times increase linearly as a function of the number of propositions in a text, even after controlling for extraneous variables (Kintsch, 1974; Haberlandt & Graesser, 1985). The slopes of the linear functions vary from 100 milliseconds to 1,500 milliseconds per proposition, depending on the reading task and the text.

Constructing Mental Models. The reader constructs the referential mental model at various levels of content, such as class-inclusion, temporality, spatiality, causality, goals, and so on. When comprehension is successful, there is coherence both *within* and *between* the levels of the mental model. Stated differently, there are no serious coherence gaps *within* a particular level and there is harmony *between* the levels of representation.

A coherence gap within the situation model occurs when a reader cannot link an incoming clause in the text to the previous content on any conceptual dimension, such as causality, temporality, spatiality, or the goals of characters (Gernsbacher, 1997; Zwaan & Radvansky, 1998). In essence, the incoming event seems to be mentioned out of the blue, so the reader needs to construct a new conceptual structure from scratch. Zwaan, Magliano and Graesser (1995) reported that reading times for clauses in text increased as a function of the number of coherence gaps along these conceptual dimensions. That is, clause-reading times were an additive function of the number of conceptual dimensions that had a coherence break (e.g., a break or discontinuity in time, space, causality, goals, agents). The extent to which clauses in text are conceptually related is an inverse function of the number of conceptual dimensions with coherence breaks (Zwaan & Radvansky, 1998; Zwaan, Langston, & Graesser, 1995).

Regarding coherence *between* levels, there needs to be a mapping between the elements of the representation at one level and the elements at another level. For example, the surface code has words and syntactic patterns that signal content features at the level of the situation model. Comprehension suffers when the surface code and mental model clash. If the text stated that "the key is turned after the cylinder rotates," there would be a discrepancy between the order of events in the situation model (the key is turned *before* the cylinder rotates) and the surface code (clause X *after* clause Y).

The comprehender obviously needs an adequate repertoire of world knowledge, domain knowledge, and cognitive skills to construct coherent representations. Comprehension breaks down when there are deficits in relevant knowledge or processing skills at particular levels of representation. When all background knowledge and skills are intact, the comprehender constructs a meaningful representation that is coherent at both local and global levels. However, when there is a deficit at a particular level of representation, the problems either propagate to other levels or, in some cases, other levels can compensate. For example, nonnative speakers of English may have trouble processing the words and syntax of English, which makes it difficult for them to process the deeper levels of representation. They might try to compensate by using their knowledge of the situation model, pragmatics, and the discourse genre to reconstruct what was being said. As another example, readers have trouble comprehending technical texts on arcane topics because they lack world knowledge about the topic. This deficit at the situation model confines their processing to the surface code and text base levels. So they might parrot back explicit information in a textbook, but have no understanding at a deeper level—a routine occurrence in our school systems. The challenge is to design the text and the testing format to encourage deeper levels of processing.

Researchers have documented some counterintuitive interactions among the text, the task, the test, and the reader's world knowledge. For example, MacNamara, Kintsch, Songer, and Kintsch (1996) investigated an interaction among (1) the readers' knowledge about a topic, (2) the coherence of the text base, and (3) the level of representation that was being tapped in a test. The readers varied in the amount of prior knowledge they had about the topic covered in the text (the topic was the functioning of the heart). Half of the readers read a text with a coherent text base; clauses were linked by appropriate connectives (*therefore, so, and*), and the topic sentences, headings, and subheadings were inserted at appropriate locations. The other half of the texts had low coherence because of violations in the insertion of connectives, topic sentences, headers and subheaders. The tests tapped either the text base level of representation (which included recall tests) or the mental-model level (which included tests of inferences and answers to deep-reasoning questions). The results of the study were not particularly surprising for the low-knowledge readers. For these readers, texts with high coherence consistently produced higher performance scores than texts with low coherence. The results were more complex for the readers with a high amount of prior knowledge about how the heart functions. A coherent text base slightly enhanced recall, but actually lowered performance on tests that tapped the mental model. The gaps in text coherence forced the high-knowledge reader to draw inferences, construct rich elaborations, and compensate by allocating more processing effort to the mental model. In essence, deep comprehension was a positive compensatory result of coherence gaps at the shallow levels of representation. Similar complex interactions among text, task, test, and knowledge have been reported in other studies (Cote, Goldman, & Saul, 1998; Graesser, Kassler, Kreuz, & Mclain-Allen, 1998; Mannes & Kintsch, 1987).

Generating Inferences. Students need to construct inferences when they construct the text base and the mental models that go beyond the information directly articulated in the text. Available research on inference generation supports the claim that many classes of inferences are routinely generated during reading when the material taps world knowledge that is familiar to the reader (Graesser, Singer, & Trabasso, 1994). In contrast, inferences are a challenge to generate when the text consists of unfamiliar scientific mechanisms (Cote et al., 1998; Graesser & Bertus, 1998; Singer, Harkness, & Moore, in press).

Table A.1 lists and defines different classes of inferences that are frequently relevant to expository texts. The inferences in Table A.2 do not exhaust the classes of inferences that comprehension researchers have investigated, but they do cover the inferences investigated frequently by researchers in discourse psychology and discourse processing. Some of the inferences are more difficult to construct than others (see the references above). For example, anaphoric and bridging inferences are made most reliably, whereas predictive inferences are very difficult to make. Explanation-based and goal inferences are prevalent in good readers, whereas poor comprehenders have a higher density of elaborative associations that are often irrelevant to the text.

Comprehension Monitoring. Good readers monitor whether they are comprehending text effectively. One counterintuitive result of comprehension research

Table A.1

Classes of Inferences That Are Relevant to Expository Texts

Anaphoric references. A pronoun or noun-phrase that refers to a previous text constituent or to an entity already introduced in the mental model.

Bridging inferences. These are any inferences that a reader needs to semantically or conceptually relate the sentence being read with the previous content. These are sometimes called *backward* inferences.

Explanation-based inferences. The event being read about is explained by a causal chain or network of previous events and states. These are sometimes called *causal antecedent* inferences.

Predictive inferences. The reader forecasts what events will causally unfold after the current event that is being read. These are sometimes called *causal consequence* or *forward* inferences.

Goal inferences. The reader infers that an agent has a motive that explains an intentional action.

Elaborative inferences. These are properties of entities, facts, and other associations that are not explained by causal mechanisms.

Process inferences. These inferences specify the detailed steps, manner, or dynamic characteristics of an event as it unfolds.

---

is that most child and adult readers have a poor ability to calibrate the success of their comprehension (Glenberg, Wilkinson, & Epstein, 1982; Hacker, Dunlosky, & Graesser, 1998). Comprehension calibration can be measured by asking readers to rate how well they comprehend a text and correlating such ratings with their comprehension scores on an objective test. These ratings are either low or modest ($r = .2$ to $.4$), which suggests that college students have disappointing comprehension calibration. Another way to calibrate comprehension is to plant contradictions in a text and to observe whether the reader detects them. Such contradictions are not detected by a surprising number of adult readers. Readers show a strong tendency to have an "illusion of comprehension" by pitching their expectations at handling the surface code, explicit text base, and other shallow levels of representation. They need to be trained to adjust their metacognitive expectations and strategies to focus on the deeper levels. This has important implications for teacher training and textbook design. There need to be adjunct aids or activities that challenge the students' misconceptions about comprehension.

Deeper-Level Comprehension Operations. It is widely acknowledged that students rarely acquire a deep understanding of the technical, expository material they are supposed to read in their courses. Students normally settle for shallow

Table A.2

Levels of Cognitive Processing and Mastery

1. *Recognition.* The process of verbatim identification of specific content (e.g., terms, facts, rules, methods, principles, procedures, objects) that was explicitly mentioned in the text

2. *Recall.* The process of actively retrieving from memory and producing content that was explicitly mentioned in the text

3. *Comprehension.* The process of demonstrating an understanding of the text at the mental-model level by generating inferences, interpreting, paraphrasing, translating, explaining, or summarizing information

4. *Application.* The process of applying knowledge extracted from text to a problem, situation, or case (fictitious or real-world) that was not explicitly mentioned in the text

5. *Analysis.* The process of decomposing elements and linking relationships between elements

6. *Synthesis.* The process of assembling new patterns and structures, such as constructing a novel solution to a problem or composing a novel message to an audience

7. *Evaluation.* The process of judging the value or effectiveness of a process, procedure, or entity, according to some criteria and standards

NOTE: Based on Bloom, 1956; Otero, Leon, & Graesser, in press.

knowledge, such as a list of concepts, a handful of facts about each concept, and simple definitions of key terms. It takes more effort and thought to acquire the difficult conceptualizations and the deep coherent explanations that would organize such shallow knowledge. The deeper knowledge is needed to fortify learners for generating inferences, solving problems, reasoning, and applying their knowledge to practical situations. The deeper levels of Bloom's (1956) taxonomy of cognitive mastery are not adequately taught, achieved, and tested in most curricula.

Table A.2 lists the major types of cognitive processes that Bloom (1956) and others proposed nearly 50 years ago. According to Bloom's taxonomy of cognitive objectives, the cognitive processes with higher numbers are more difficult and require greater depth of thinking. Recognition and recall are the easiest processes, comprehension falls in the middle, and processes 4–7 are the most difficult. It is debatable whether there are differences in difficulty among categories 4–7, so most applications of this taxonomy collapse them into one category.

Navigation. Particularly for electronic texts, an additional skill that we call *navigation* becomes important. This skill consists of knowing how to access hyperlinks as well as knowing how to move forward and backward in electronic text.

CONSEQUENCES

The consequences of reading, or comprehension outcomes, are, of course, the aspect of the reading instruction activity of greatest interest to members of the RRSG, and the aspect in which variability is the most puzzling and the most distressing. A difficulty in discussing consequences in any great detail is that only very limited assessments of reading comprehension are available. The assessments that exist tend to operationalize comprehension in an impoverished way, focusing on knowledge outcomes over application and engagement outcomes. They also tend to reflect consequences associated with reading particular texts rather than consequences more broadly defined, such as learning some new vocabulary items or new meanings for previously known words, bringing a previously held viewpoint into question, enhancing the reader's understanding of how to present a convincing argument, or drawing conclusions about the writer's political biases. Until comprehension measures expand to reflect an underlying theory that acknowledges a variety of possible consequences, both immediate and long term, we will be severely hampered in our capacities to engage in excellent research on this topic.

OUTLINE OF A SAMPLE REQUEST FOR APPLICATION

The analyses and judgments of the RRSG that constitute the body of this report are intended to provide broad guidance for creating a program of research and development that will support the improvement of reading comprehension instruction in U.S. schools. However, this broad guidance is not sufficient for actually providing instructions to potential applicants for funding. Funding agencies that intend to support such R&D will need to write specific requests for applications (RFAs) that delineate narrower areas of R&D that the funding is intended to support and that provide more explicit guidance to the applicants.

In this appendix, the RRSG has illustrated its own sense of what would constitute the core of an effective RFA in a single area—assessment. We chose assessment because advances in assessment are crucial to effective R&D related to reading comprehension. If time had permitted, we would have also developed similar core RFAs in several other areas identified in the body of the report including (1) improving instruction using currently available knowledge; (2) developing new knowledge to inform more radical changes in instruction; (3) enhancing teacher preparation and professional development; (4) gaining a better understanding of the properties of reader-text interactions through studies using various genres of text as well as comparisons of electronic and linear texts; and (5) exploring the impact of technology on reading comprehension, reading activities being undertaken by learners, and opportunities for instruction.

The example that follows[1] should probably be viewed as a starting point. Any funding agency would want to elaborate on this RFA, perhaps by including a review of the literature, a more detailed specification of research goals, examples of possible R&D activities, funding levels, and so on. The proposal includes examples of short-, mid-, and long-term projects, and a funding agency, such as OERI, might choose to address these in separate RFAs issued at different points in time.

---

[1]In this example, we have drawn heavily on material in earlier chapters of this report.

However, the core content we have provided here seems to us to convey the key points and spirit of what we view as being important in guiding potential applicants for work on assessment of reading comprehension.

REQUEST FOR APPLICATIONS IN THE DOMAIN OF ASSESSMENT

Statement of the Problem

Currently available assessments of student performance in the field of reading comprehension are a persistent source of complaints from both practitioners and researchers. These complaints claim that the assessments

- inadequately represent the complexity of the target domain

- conflate comprehension with vocabulary, domain-specific knowledge, word-reading ability, and other reader capacities involved in comprehension

- do not reflect an understanding of reading comprehension as a developmental process or as a product of instruction

- do not examine the assumptions underlying the relationship of successful performance to the dominant group's interests and values

- are not useful for teachers

- tend to narrow the curriculum

- are one-dimensional and method-dependent, and often fail to address even minimal criteria for reliability and validity.

Indeed, most currently used comprehension assessments reflect the purpose for which such assessments were originally developed—to sort children on a single dimension by using a single method. More important, though, is that none of the currently available comprehension assessments is based in a viable or articulated theory of comprehension. Because currently used comprehension instruments are all unsatisfactory in various ways, the field has not selected a common standard for assessing comprehension. Until instrumentation and operationalization of comprehension is widely agreed on, mounting a truly programmatic research effort will be difficult.

These considerations, as well as current thinking about the nature of reading comprehension (see the body of this report), create a demand for new kinds of assessment strategies and instruments that more robustly reflect the dynamic, developmental nature of comprehension and represent adequately the interactions among the dimensions of reader, activity, text, and context.

Currently, widely used comprehension assessments focus heavily on only a few tasks: reading for immediate recall, reading for gist, and reading to infer or disambiguate word meaning. Assessment procedures to evaluate learners' capacities to modify old or build new knowledge structures, to use information acquired while reading in the interest of problem solving, to evaluate texts on particular criteria, or to become absorbed in reading and develop affective or aesthetic responses to text have occasionally been developed in the pursuit of particular research programs, but they have not influenced standard assessment practices. Because knowledge, application, and engagement are the crucial consequences of reading with comprehension, assessments that reflect all three are needed. Further, the absence of attention to these consequences in widely used reading assessments diminishes the emphasis on them in instructional practices as well.

Because existing measures of comprehension fail to reflect adequately the inherent complexities of the comprehension process, they limit the kinds of research that can be done and undermine optimal instruction. Good assessment tools are crucial to conducting sensible research. In addition, though, as long as we define comprehension by default as reading a passage and answering a few multiple-choice questions about it, teachers will have little incentive to instruct children in ways that reflect a deeper and more accurate conceptualization of the construct.

Efforts have been made to develop measures of comprehension that are referenced to the characteristics of text, that is, a way of relating an assessment of comprehension to the difficulty of the text. Although such measures (e.g., Lexile) provide information that supports instruction by indicating a child's level of comprehension, different estimates of readability do not correspond well with one another. Moreover, they provide no diagnostic information for individualizing instruction, nor do efforts such as the Lexile text system fit easily into a larger assessment system.

Requirements for the Assessment System to Be Developed

A comprehensive assessment program that reflects the current thinking about reading comprehension must satisfy many requirements that have not been addressed by any assessment instruments, while also satisfying the standard psychometric criteria (e.g., reliability and validity). A list of requirements for such a system includes, at a minimum, the following:

- *Capacity to reflect authentic outcomes.* Although any particular assessment may not reflect the full array of consequences, the inclusion of a wider array than that currently being tested is crucial. For example, students' beliefs about reading and about themselves as readers may constitute supports or obstacles to their optimal development as comprehenders; teachers may benefit enormously from having ways to elicit and assess such beliefs.

- *Congruence between assessments and the processes involved in comprehension.* Assessments must be available that target particular operations involved in comprehension, in the interest of revealing inter- and intra-individual differences that might inform our understanding of the comprehension process and of outcome differences. The dimensionality of the instruments in relation to theory should be clearly apparent.

- *Developmental sensitivity.* Any assessment system needs to be sensitive across the full developmental range of interest and to reflect developmentally central phenomena related to comprehension. Assessments of young children's reading tend to depend on the child's level of word reading and must control for the level of decoding to assess comprehension adequately. The available listening comprehension assessments for young children do not reflect their rich oral language processing capacities, discourse skills, or even the full complexity of their sentence processing.

- *Capacity to identify individual children as poor comprehenders.* An effective assessment system should be able to identify individual children as poor comprehenders, not only in terms of prerequisite skills such as fluency in word identification and decoding, but also in terms of cognitive deficits and gaps in relevant knowledge (e.g., background and domain specific) that might adversely affect reading and comprehension, even in children who have adequate word-level skills. It is also critically important that such a system provide for the early identification of children who are apt to encounter difficulties in reading comprehension because of limited resources to carry out one or another operation involved in comprehension.

- *Capacity to identify subtypes of poor comprehenders.* Reading comprehension is a complex process. It therefore follows that comprehension difficulties could come about because of deficiencies in one or another of the components of comprehension specified in the model. Thus, an effective assessment system should have the means to identify subtypes of poor comprehenders in terms of the components and the desired outcomes of comprehension and in terms of both intra- and inter-individual differences in acquiring the knowledge and skills necessary for becoming a good comprehender.

- *Instructional sensitivity.* The major purposes for assessments are to inform instruction and to reflect the effect of instruction or intervention. Thus, an effective assessment system should provide not only important information about a child's relative standing in appropriate normative populations (school, state, or national norms groups), but also important information about a child's relative strengths and weaknesses for purposes of educational planning.

- *Openness to intra-individual differences.* Understanding the performance of an individual often requires attending to differences in performance across activities with varying purposes and with a variety of texts and types of text.

- *Utility for instructional decisionmaking.* Assessments can inform instructional practice if they are designed to identify domains that instruction might target, rather than to provide summary scores useful only for comparison with other learners' scores. Another aspect of utility for instructional decisionmaking is the transparency of the information provided by the test given to teachers who are not technically trained.

- *Adaptability with respect to individual, social, linguistic, and cultural variation.* Good tests of reading comprehension, of listening comprehension, and of oral language production target authentic outcomes and reflect key component processes. If performance on the task reflects differences owing to individual, social, linguistic, or cultural variation that are not directly related to reading comprehension performance, the tests are inadequate for the purposes of the research agenda proposed here.

- *A basis in measurement theory and psychometrics.* This aspect should address reliability within scales and over time, as well as multiple components of validity at the item level, concurrently with other measures, and predictively relative to the longer-term development of reading proficiency. Studies of the dimensionality of the instruments in relationship to the theory underlying their construction are particularly important. Test construction and the evaluation of instruments are important areas of investigation and highly relevant to the proposed research agenda.

Clearly, no single assessment will meet all these criteria. Instead, this RFA seeks work that will build toward an integrated system of assessments, some of which may be particularly appropriate for particular groups (e.g., emergent or beginning readers, older struggling readers, second-language readers, or readers with a particular interest in dinosaurs). Furthermore, the various assessments included in the system will address different purposes (e.g., a portmanteau assessment for accountability or screening purposes, diagnostic assessments for guiding intervention, curriculum-linked assessments for guiding instruction, and so forth). Given that multiple assessments are proposed, studies of their dimensionality and the interrelations of these dimensions across measures are especially critical.

Research Plans

Responses to this RFA should take the following issues into account. We seek a mix of large- and small-scale efforts and a mix of short- and long-term efforts. We will consider an application more positively if it builds into the work plan mechanisms for developing the expertise of doctoral and young postdoctoral scholars in the psychometric and content areas relevant to assessing reading comprehension. Applications that have an assessment agenda embedded within another research undertaking (e.g., evaluating the effectiveness of an intervention or developing model teacher education efforts) will be considered for co-funding.

A variety of activities will be considered for funding under this initiative. A few examples for short-, medium-, and long-term research efforts are provided below. These examples are meant to stimulate thinking and are not an exhaustive list of the possible relevant kinds of activities. Consideration of the reliability, validity, and dimensionality of different assessment instruments and approaches is essential to all these endeavors.

Examples of Short-Term Activities

- Generate an inventory of available tests purporting to assess comprehension and evaluate them on the requirements indicated above. Mechanisms for carrying out this activity might include a panel who would provide a consensus or an empirically driven evaluation, or a research effort to review the available norms, which would then generate cross-test reliability data.

- Generate an inventory of and evaluate the assessment strategies, tools, and instruments that teachers, schools, districts, and states are using and the ways that teachers use the information collected within classrooms or schools. Again, the specific mechanism for carrying out this activity might include a panel of assessment officers from states and large districts, a teacher survey, or observational research in a stratified sample of schools.

- Generate an inventory of and evaluate what pre-service teachers learn about the assessment of reading comprehension. A survey of teacher education institutions, an analysis of syllabi and texts used widely in teacher education programs, interview studies with teacher educators, or other mechanisms might be used to address this need.

- Use established databases to evaluate the reliability, validity, and dimensionality of existing assessments of reading comprehension.

Examples of Medium-Term Activities

- Use the information gathered on which instruments are good for what purpose to develop assessments of lesser-studied domains. Such assessments will be useful in instructional settings and will differentiate the relative contribution that variations among readers make to an overall level of performance. For example:

  — discourse structure, including genre

  — understanding written syntax

  — mental model construction—content segmentation

  — metacognitive strategy use

  — vocabulary.

  Developing these measures ultimately will enable researchers to look at the similarity of comprehension operations across a variety of text types and of content.

- Develop measures that reflect engagement and the application of knowledge as consequences of comprehension in order to relate those consequences to the more commonly studied ones of (often temporary) knowledge accumulation. Such measures could then also serve as a research agenda for seeking to understand how interest or motivation affects the reading comprehension process and could be used by teachers to select optimally engaging texts for instructing their struggling students.

- Assess systematically the effect of various accommodations for second-language readers on comprehension outcome measures. Accommodations to be tested might include various manipulations of the text (simplified syntax, modified rhetorical structures, access to translations of key words), manipulations of preparation for reading (providing background knowledge in first-language reading or pre-teaching key vocabulary with translations), or manipulations of response modes (responding in the first language or responding with support from a first-language dictionary).

- Evaluate systematically the dimensions measured by different assessments in relation to more traditional assessments and the proposed new approaches to assessment. How well does the dimensionality map onto the theories underlying the development of the assessments?

Examples of Long-Term Activities

- Use the accumulated information about what assessments are available and how they might be well used to develop professional training for teachers and other decisionmakers in how to interpret and use assessment data optimally.

- Collate information from several states or large districts that are using comparable and adequate assessments of reading comprehension to establish benchmarks for appropriate progress in reading comprehension and determine scores that reflect those benchmarks on a variety of measures. This would be a first step in formulating a detailed picture of how serious the problem of comprehension achievement in the United States really is.

REFERENCES

Adams, M. J. (1990). Beginning to read: Thinking and learning about print. Cambridge, MA: MIT Press.

Alexander, P. A., & Jetton, T. (2000). Learning from text: A multidimensional and developmental perspective. In M. L. Kamil, P. B. Mosenthal, P. D. Pearson, & R. Barr (Eds.), Handbook of reading research: Volume III (pp. 285–310). Mahwah, NJ: Erlbaum.

Alexander, P. A., & Murphy, P. K. (1998). Profiling the differences in students' knowledge, interest, and strategic processing. Journal of Educational Psychology, 90(3), 435–447.

Allington, R. L. (1983). The reading instruction provided readers of differing reading abilities. Elementary School Journal, 83, 548–559.

Allington, R. L., & McGill-Franzen, A. (1989). School response to reading failure: Chapter I and special education students in grades 2, 4, and 8. Elementary School Journal, 89, 529–542.

Alvermann, D. E. (2001). Effective literacy instruction for adolescents. Chicago: National Reading Conference.

Alvermann, D. E., Hagood, M. C., Heron, A. H., Hughes, P., Williams, K. B., & Jun, Y. (2000). After-school media clubs for reluctant adolescent readers (Final report to the Spencer Foundation, Grant #199900278). Chicago: Spencer Foundation.

Anders, P. L., Hoffman, J. V., & Duffy, G. G. (2000). Teaching teachers to teach reading: Paradigm shifts, persistent problems, and challenges. In M. L. Kamil, P. B. Mosenthal, P. D. Pearson, & R. Barr (Eds.), Handbook of reading research: Volume III (pp. 719–742). Mahwah, NJ: Erlbaum.

Anglin, J. M. (1993). Vocabulary development: A morphological analysis. Monographs of the Society for Research in Child Development, 58(10), 1–166.

Armbruster, B. B., & Anderson, T. H. (1984). Structures of explanations in history textbooks or so what if Governor Stanford missed the spike and hit the rail? Journal of Curriculum Studies, 16(2), 181–194.

Armbruster, B. B., & Armstrong, J. O. (1993). Locating information in text: A focus on children in the elementary grades. Contemporary Educational Psychology, 18(2), 139–161.

Baddeley, A. D. (1986). Working memory. London: Oxford University Press.

Baddeley, A. D., & Logie, R. H. (1999). Working memory: The multiple component. In I. A. Miyake & P. Shah (Eds.), Models of working memory: Mechanisms of active maintenance and executive control (pp. 28–61). New York: Cambridge University Press.

Balcytiene, A. (1999). Exploring individual processes of knowledge construction with hypertext. Instructional Science, 27(3–4), 303–328.

Barkley, R. A. (1990). Attention deficit hyperactivity disorder. New York: Guilford Press.

Barton, D., Hamilton, M., & Ivanic, R. (Eds.). (2000). Situated literacies. New York: Routledge.

Baumann, J., Hoffman, J., Moon, J., & Duffy-Hester, A. M. (1998). Where are teachers' voices in the phonics/whole language debate? Results from a survey of U.S. elementary teachers. The Reading Teacher, 51, 636–652.

Beach, R., & Lundell, D. (1998). Early adolescents' use of computer-mediated communication in writing and reading. In D. Reinking, M. McKenna, L. Labbo, & R. Kieffer (Eds.), Handbook of literacy and technology: Transformations in a post-typographic world (pp. 323–341). Mahwah, NJ: Erlbaum.

Beck, I. L., & McKeown, M. G. (2001). Text talk: Capturing the benefits of read-aloud experiences for young children, Reading Teacher, 55(1), 10–20.

Beck, I. L., McKeown, M. G., Hamilton, R. L., & Kucan, L. (1997). Questioning the author: An approach for enhancing student engagement with text. Newark, DE: International Reading Association.

Beck, I. L., McKeown, M. G., Sinatra, G. M., & Loxterman, J. A. (1991). Revising social studies text from a text-processing perspective: Evidence of improved comprehensibility. Reading Research Quarterly, 26(3), 251–276.

Beck, I. L., Perfetti, C. A., & McKeown, M. G. (1982). Effects of long-term vocabulary instruction on lexical access and reading comprehension. Journal of Educational Psychology, 74(4), 506–521.

Begg, I., & Clark, J. M. (1975). Contextual imagery in meaning and memory. Memory & Cognition, 3, 117–122.

Begg, I., Upfold, D., & Wilton, T. D. (1978). Imagery in verbal communication. Journal of Mental Imagery, 2, 165–186.

Bernhardt, E. (2000). Second-language reading as a case study of reading scholarship in the 20th century. In M. L. Kamil, P. B. Mosenthal, P. D. Pearson, & R. Barr (Eds.), Handbook of reading research: Volume III (pp. 793–811). Mahwah, NJ: Erlbaum.

Berninger, V. W., Abbott, R. D., Billingsley, F., & Nagy, W. (in press). Processes underlying timing and fluency of reading: Efficiency, automaticity, coordination, and morphological awareness. In M. Wolf (Ed.), Dyslexia, fluency, and the brain. Timonium, MD: York Press.

Berninger, V. W., Abbott, R., Brooksher, R., Lemos, Z., Ogier, S., Zook, D., & Mostafapour, E. (in press). A connectionist approach to making the predictability of English orthography explicit to at-risk beginning readers: Evidence of alternative, effective strategies. Developmental Neuropsychology.

Biber, D. (1988). Variation across speech and writing. Cambridge, MA: Cambridge University Press.

Blachman, B. A. (1997). Foundations of reading acquisition and dyslexia. Mahwah, NJ: Erlbaum.

Blachowicz, C., & Ogle, D. (2001). Reading Comprehension. New York: The Guilford Press.

Bloom, B. S. (1956). Taxonomy of educational objectives. Handbook I: Cognitive domain. New York: McKay.

Boyle, J. R., & Weishaar, M. (1997). The effects of expert-generated versus student-generated cognitive organizers on the reading comprehension of students with learning disabilities. Learning Disabilities Research and Practice, 12(4), 228–235.

Bradley, L., & Bryant, P. E. (1983). Categorizing sounds and learning to read: A causal connection. Nature, 303, 419–421.

Bransford, J., Brown, A., & Cocking, R. R. (1999). How people learn: Brain, mind, experience, and school. Washington, DC: National Academy Press.

Bransford, J. D., Goldman, S. R., & Vye, N. J. (1991). Making a difference in people's abilities to think: Reflections on a decade of work and some hopes for the future. In L. Okagaki & R. J. Sternberg (Eds.), Directors of development: Influences on the development of children's thinking (pp. 147–180). Hillsdale, NJ: Erlbaum.

Breznitz, Z. (in press). The role of inter-modality temporal features of speed of information processing in asynchrony between visual-orthographic and auditory-phonological processing. In M. Wolf (Ed.), Dyslexia, fluency, and the brain. Timonium, MD: York Press.

Broadbent, D. E. (1958). Perception and communication. New York: Oxford University Press.

Brooks, C., & Warren, R. P. (1972). Modern rhetoric. New York: Harcourt Brace Jovanovich.

Brown, A. L. (1997). Transforming schools into communities of thinking and learning about serious matters. American Psychologist, 52, 399–414.

Brown, A. L., & Campione, J. C. (1994). Guided discovery in a community of learners. In K. McGilly (Ed.), Classroom lessons: Integrating cognitive theory and classroom practice (pp. 229–270). Cambridge, MA: MIT Press.

Brown, R., Pressley, M., Van Meter, P., & Schuder, T. (1996). A quasi-experimental validation of transactional strategies instruction with low-achieving second-grade readers. Journal of Educational Psychology, 88(1), 18–37.

Buenning, M., & Tollefson, N. (1987). The cultural gap hypothesis as an explanation for the achievement patterns of Mexican-American students. Psychology in the Schools, 24(3), 264–272.

Burke, S. M., Pflaum, S. W., & Knafle, J. D. (1982). The influence of Black English on diagnosis of reading in learning disabled and normal readers. Journal of Learning Disabilities, 15, 19–22.

Campbell, J. R., Hombo, C. M., & Mazzeo, J. (2000). NAEP 1999 trends in academic progress: Three decades of student performance. Washington, DC: National Center for Education Statistics, U.S. Department of Education.

Cantor, J., Engle, R. W., & Hamilton, G. (1991). Short-term memory, working memory, and verbal abilities: How do they relate? Intelligence, 15, 229–246.

Carlisle, J. F. (1995). Morphological awareness and early reading achievement. In L. B. Feldman (Ed.), Morphological aspects of language processing (pp. 189–209). Hillsdale, NJ: Erlbaum.

Carpenter, P. A., Miyake, A., & Just, M. A. (1994). Working memory constraints in comprehension: Evidence from individual differences, aphasia, and aging. In M. A. Gernsbacher (Ed.), Handbook of psycholinguistics (pp. 1075–1122). San Diego, CA: Academic Press.

Carver, R. P. (1992). What do standardized tests of reading comprehension measure in terms of efficiency, accuracy, and rate? Reading Research Quarterly, 27(4), 346–359.

Cazden, C. (1988). Classroom discourse: The language of teaching and learning. Portsmouth, NH: Heinemann.

Chafe, W., & Tannen, D. (1987). The relation between written and spoken language. Annual Review of Anthropology, 16, 383–407.

Chall, J. S., Jacobs, V. A., & Baldwin, L. E. (1990). The reading crisis: Why poor children fall behind. Cambridge, MA: Harvard University Press.

Chambliss, M. J. (in press). The characteristics of well-designed science textbooks. In J. Otero, J. A. Leon, & A. C. Graesser (Eds.), The psychology of science text comprehension. Mahwah, NJ: Erlbaum.

Chan, L. K., & Cole, P. G. (1986). The effects of comprehension monitoring training on the reading competence of learning disabled and regular class students. RASE: Remedial & Special Education, 7(4), 33–40.

Chan, L. K., Cole, P. G., & Barfett, S. (1987). Comprehension monitoring: Detection and identification of text inconsistencies by LD and normal students. Learning Disability Quarterly, 10(2), 114–124.

Cochran-Smith, M., & Lytle, S. (1999). Relationship of knowledge and practice: Teacher learning in communities. In A. Iran-Nejad & C. D. Pearson (Eds.), Review of research in education (Vol. 24, pp. 249–306). Washington, DC: American Educational Research Association.

Cohen, D. K., & Ball, D. L. (1990). Policy and practice: An overview. Educational Evaluation and Policy Analysis, 12(3), 347–353.

Cote, N., Goldman, S. R., & Saul, E. U. (1998). Students making sense of informational text: Relations between processing and representation. Discourse-Processes, 25, 1–53.

Cremin, L. A. (1965). The genius of American education. Pittsburgh, PA: University of Pittsburgh Press.

Cuban, L. (1993). How teachers taught. New York: Teachers College Press.

Curtis, M. E. (1980). Development of components of reading skill. Journal of Educational Psychology, 72, 656–669.

Daneman, M., & Carpenter, P. A. (1980). Individual differences in working memory and reading. Journal of Verbal Learning and Verbal Behavior, 19, 450–466.

Darling-Hammond, L. (1990). Achieving our goals: Superficial or structural reforms? Phi Delta Kappan, 72(4), 286–295.

Darling-Hammond, L. (2000). Teacher quality and student achievement: A review of state policy evidence. Educational Policy Analysis Archives, 8(1), 1–42.

Darling-Hammond, L., & Green, J. (1994). Teacher quality and equality. In J. Goodlad & P. Keating (Eds.), Access to knowledge. New York: College Entrance Examination Board.

Davidson-Shivers, G. V., Rasmussen, K. L., & Bratton-Jeffery, M. F. (1997). Investigating learning strategies generation in a hypermedia environment using qualitative methods. Journal of Computing in Childhood Education, 8(2/3), 247–261.

Davis, F. B. (1944). Fundamental factors in reading. Psychometrica, 9, 185–197.

Davis, F. B. (1968). Research in comprehension in reading. Reading Research Quarterly, 3, 499–545.

Davis, F. B. (1972). Psychometric research on comprehension in reading. Reading Research Quarterly, 7, 628–678.

Davison, A., & Kantor, R. (1982). On the failure of readability formulas to define readable texts: A case study from adaptations. Reading Research Quarterly, 17(2), 187–209.

de Castell, S. (1996). On finding one's place in the text: Literacy as a technology of self-formation. In W. F. Pinar (Ed.), Contemporary curriculum discourses: Twenty years of JCT (pp. 398–411). New York: Peter Lang.

Dickinson, D. K., & DeTemple, J. (1998). Putting parents in the picture: Maternal reports of preschoolers' literacy as a predictor of early reading. Early Childhood Research Quarterly, 13, 241–261.

Dickinson, D. K., & Snow, C. E. (1987). Interrelationships among prereading and oral language skills in kindergartners from two social classes. Early Childhood Research Quarterly, 2, 1–25.

Dickinson, D. K., & Sprague, K. E. (2001). The nature and impact of early childhood care environments on the language and early literacy development of children from low-income families. In S. B. Neuman & D. K. Dickinson (Eds.), Handbook of early literacy research (pp. 263–280). New York: The Guilford Press.

Dickinson, D. K., & Tabors, P. O. (Eds.). (2001). Beginning literacy with language: Young children learning at home and school. Baltimore: Brookes Publishing.

Dillon, D. R. (1989). Showing them that I want them to learn and that I care about who they are: A microethnography of the social organization of a secondary low-track English classroom. American Educational Research Journal, 26, 227–259.

Dixon-Krauss, L. A. (1995). Partner reading and writing: Peer social dialogue and the zone of proximal development. Journal of Reading Behavior, 27(1), 45–63.

Dole, J. A., Valencia, S. W., Greer, E. A., & Wardrop, J. L. (1991). Effects of two types of prereading instruction on the comprehension of narrative and expository text. Reading Research Quarterly, 26, 142–159.

Duffy, G. G., Roehler, L. R., Sivan, E., Rackliffe, G., Book, C., Meloth, M. S., Vavrus, L. G., Wesselman, R., Putnam, J., & Bassiri, D. (1987). Effects of explaining the reasoning associated with using reading strategies. Reading Research Quarterly, 22(3), 347–368.

Duke, N. K. (2000). For the rich it's richer: Print environments and experiences offered to first-grade students in very low- and very high-SES school districts. American Educational Research Journal, 37, 456–457.

Durkin, D. (1978–79). What classroom observations reveal about reading comprehension instruction. Reading Research Quarterly, 14(4), 481–533.

Eccles, J. S., Wigfield, A., & Schiefele, U. (1998). Motivation to succeed. In N. Eisenberg (Vol. Ed.), Handbook of child psychology: Vol. 3, Social, emotional and personality development (5th ed., pp. 1017–1095). New York: Wiley.

Elley, W. B. (1991). Acquiring literacy in a second language: The effect of book-based programs. Language Learning, 41(3), 375–411.

Elmore, R. F. (1999–2000). Building a new structure for school leadership. American Educator, 23(4), 6–13.

Engle, R. W., Cantor, J., & Carullo, J. J. (1992). Individual differences in working memory and comprehension: A test of four hypotheses. Journal of Experimental Psychology: Learning, Memory, and Cognition, 18, 972–992.

Engle, R. W., Tuholski, S. W., Laughlin, J. E., & Conway, A. R. (1999). Working memory, short-term memory, and fluid intelligence: A latent variable approach. Journal of Experimental Psychology: General, 128, 309–331.

Erickson, F. (1992). Ethnographic microanalysis of interaction. In M. D. LeCompte, W. L. Millroy, & J. Preissle (Eds.), The handbook of qualitative research in education (pp. 201–225). London: Academic Press.

Ericsson, K. A., & Kintsch, W. (1995). Long-term working memory. Psychological Review, 102, 211–245.

Eviatar, Z., & Ibrahim, R. (2000). Bilingual is as bilingual does: Metalinguistic abilities of Arabic-speaking children. Applied Psycholinguistics, 21(4), 451–471.

Faulkner, H. J., & Levy, B. A. (1999). Fluent and nonfluent forms of transfer in reading: Words and their message. Psychonomic Bulletin & Review, 6(1), 111–116.

Ferguson, R. F. (1991). Paying for public education: New evidence on how and why money matters. Harvard Journal of Legislation, 28(2), 465–498.

Fischer, U. (1994). Learning words from context and dictionaries: An experimental comparison. Applied Psycholinguistics, 15(4), 551–574.

Fisher, C. J., Fox, D. I., & Paille, E. (1996). Teacher education research in the English language arts and reading. In J. Sikula, T. J. Buttery, & E. Guyton (Eds.), Handbook of research on teacher education (2nd ed., pp. 410–441). New York: Macmillan.

Fletcher J. M., Shaywitz, S. E., Shankweiler, D. P., Katz, L., Liberman, I. Y., Steubing, K. K., Francis, D. J., Fowler, A. E. & Shaywitz, B. A. (1994). Cognitive profiles of reading disability: Comparisons of discrepancy and low achievement definitions. Journal of Educational Psychology, 86, 6–23.

Fodor, J. A., Bever, T. G., & Garrett, M. F. (1974). The psychology of language: An introduction to psycholinguistics and generative grammar. New York: McGraw-Hill.

Freebody, P., & Anderson, R. C. (1983). Effects of vocabulary difficulty, text cohesion, and schema availability on reading comprehension. Reading Research Quarterly, 18(3), 277–294.

Freire, P. (1970). Pedagogy of the oppressed. New York: Continuum.

Fuchs, L. S., Fuchs, D., Hosp, M. K., & Jenkins, J. R. (2001). Oral reading fluency as an indicator of reading competence: A theoretical, empirical and historical analysis. Scientific Studies of Reading, 5(3), 239–256.

Fukkink, R. G., & de Glopper, K. (1998). Effects of instruction in deriving word meaning from context: A meta-analysis. Review of Educational Research, 68(4), 450–469.

Fullan, M. G. (1992). Successful school improvement: The implementation perspective and beyond. Bristol, PA: Open University Press.

Galda, L., & Beach, R. (2001). Response to literature as a cultural activity. Reading Research Quarterly, 36, 64–73.

García, G. E. (1991). Factors influencing the English reading test performance of Spanish-speaking Hispanic children. Reading Research Quarterly, 26(4), 371–392.

García, G. E. (2000). Bilingual children's reading. In M. Kamil, P. Rosenthal, P. D. Pearson, & R. Barr (Eds.), Handbook of reading research: Volume III (pp. 813–834). Mahwah, NJ: Erlbaum.

García, G. E., & Nagy, W. E. (1993). Latino students' concept of cognates. National Reading Conference Yearbook, 42, 367–373.

García, G. E., Pearson, P. D., & Jiménez, R. T. (1994). The at-risk situation: A synthesis of reading research (A special report). Champaign, IL: Center for the Study of Reading, University of Illinois.

Gaskins, I. W. (1998). There's more to teaching at-risk and delayed readers than good reading instruction. The Reading Teacher, 51, 534–547.

Gaskins, I. W., Anderson, R. C., Pressley, M., Cunicelli, E. A., & Satlow, E. (1993). Six teachers' dialogue during cognitive process instruction. The Elementary School Journal, 93, 277–304.

Gaskins, I. W., & Elliot, T. T. (1991) Implementing cognitive strategy instruction across the school: The Benchmark manual for teachers. Cambridge, MA: Brookline Books.

Gee, J. (1990). Social linguistics and literacies: Ideology in discourses. London: The Falmer Press.

Gernsbacher, M. A. (1997). Two decades of structure building. Discourse Processes, 23, 265–304.

Gersten, R., Fuchs, L. S., Williams, J. P., & Baker, S. (in press). Teaching reading comprehension strategies to students with learning disabilities: A review of research. Review of Educational Research.

Gillingham, M. G., Garner, R., Guthrie, J. T., & Sawyer, R. (1989). Children's control of computer-based reading assistance in answering synthesis questions. Computers in Human Behavior, 5(1), 61–75.

Glenberg, A. M., Wilkinson, A. A., & Epstein, W. (1982). The illusion of knowing: Failure in the assessment of comprehension. Memory & Cognition, 10, 597–602.

Goldenberg, C. (2001). Making schools work for low-income families in the 21st century. In S. B. Neuman & D. K. Dickinson (Eds.), Handbook of early literacy research (pp. 211–231). New York: The Guilford Press.

Gough, P. B., & Tunmer, W. E. (1986). Decoding, reading, and reading disability. Remedial and Special Education, 7, 6–10.

Graesser, A. C., & Bertus, E. L. (1998). The construction of causal inferences while reading expository texts on science and technology. Scientific Studies of Reading, 2, 247–269.

Graesser, A. C., Bowers, C., Olde, B., & Pomeroy, V. (1999). Who said what? Source memory for narrator and character agents in literary short stories. Journal of Educational Psychology, 91, 284–300.

Graesser, A. C., Kassler, M. A., Kreuz, R. J., & Mclain-Allen, B. (1998). Verification of statements about story worlds that deviate from normal conceptions of time: What is true about Einstein's dreams. Cognitive Psychology, 35, 246–301.

Graesser, A. C., Millis, K., & Zwaan, R. A. (1997). Discourse comprehension. Annual Review of Psychology, 48, 163–189.

Graesser, A. C., Singer, M., & Trabasso, T. (1994). Constructing inferences during narrative text comprehension. Psychological Review, 101(3), 371–395.

Graves, M. F. (2000). A vocabulary program to complement and bolster a middle-grade comprehension program. In B. M. Taylor, M. F. Graves, & P. van den Broek (Eds.), Reading for meaning: Fostering comprehension in the middle grades. Newark, DE: International Reading Association.

Graves, M. F., Cooke, C. L., & LaBerge, M. J. (1983). Effects of previewing short stories. Reading Research Quarterly, 18, 262–276.

Graves, M. F., & Graves, B. B. (1994). Scaffolding reading experiences: Designs for student success. Norwood, MA: Christopher-Gordon.

Graves, M. F., Graves, B. B., & Braaten, S. (1996). Scaffolded reading experiences for inclusive classrooms. Educational Leadership, 53(5), 14–16.

Graves, M. F., & Slater, W. H. (1996). Vocabulary instruction in content areas. In D. Lapp, J. Flood, & N. Farnan (Eds.), Content area reading and learning instructional strategies (2nd ed., pp. 261–275). Boston: Allyn & Bacon.

Graves, M. F., Watts-Taffe, S. M., & Graves, B. B. (1998). Essentials of elementary reading. Needham Heights, MA: Allyn & Bacon.

Guthrie, J. T., Cox, K. E., Anderson, E., Harris, K., Mazzoni, S., & Rach, L. (1998). Principles of integrated instruction for engagement in reading. Educational Psychology Review, 10(2), 177–199.

Guthrie, J. T., Van Meter, P., Hancock, G. R., Alao, S., Anderson, E., & McCann, A. (1998). Does concept oriented reading instruction increase strategy use and conceptual learning from text? Journal of Educational Psychology, 90(2), 261–278.

Guthrie, J. T., & Wigfield, A. (2000). Engagement and motivation in reading. In M. L. Kamil, P. B. Mosenthal, P. D. Pearson, & R. Barr (Eds.), Handbook of reading research: Volume III (pp. 403–422). Mahwah, NJ: Erlbaum.

Guthrie, J. T., Wigfield, A., & VonSecker, C. (2000). Effects of integrated instruction on motivation and strategy use in reading. Journal of Educational Psychology, 92(2), 331–341.

Gyselinck, V., & Tardieu, H. (1999). The role of illustrations in text comprehension: What, when, for whom and why? In H. van Oostendorp & S. R. Goldman (Eds.), The construction of mental representations during reading (pp. 195–218). Mahwah, NJ: Erlbaum.

Haberlandt, K., & Graesser, A. C. (1985). Component processes in text comprehension and some of their interactions. Journal of Experimental Psychology: General, 114, 357–374.

Hacker, D. J., Dunlosky, J., & Graesser, A. C. (Eds.). (1998). Metacognition in educational theory and practice. Mahwah, NJ: Erlbaum.

Heath, S. B. (1981). What no bedtime story means: Narrative skills at home and school. Language in Society, 11, 49–76.

Heath, S. B. (1982). Questioning at home and school: A comparative study. In G. Spindler (Ed.), Doing the ethnography of schooling: Educational anthropology in action (pp. 102–131). New York: Holt, Rinehart, & Winston.

Hegarty, M., Carpenter, P. A., & Just, M. A. (1991). Diagrams in the comprehension of scientific texts. In R. Barr, M. Kamil, P. Mosenthal, & P. D. Pearson (Eds.), Handbook of reading research: Volume II (pp. 641–668). New York: Longman.

Hernandez, H. (1989). Multicultural education: A teachers' guide to content and process. New York: Merrill.

Hiebert, E. H., & Martin, L. A. (2001). The texts of beginning reading instruction. In S. B. Neuman & D. K. Dickinson (Eds.), Handbook of early literacy research (pp. 361–376). New York: The Guilford Press.

Hiebert, E. H., & Rafael, T. E. (1996). Psychological perspectives on literacy and extensions to educational practice. In D. C. Berliner & R. C. Calfee (Eds.), Handbook of educational psychology. New York: Macmillan.

Hoover, W., & Gough, P. B. (1990). The simple view of reading. Reading and Writing: An Interdisciplinary Journal, 2, 127–160.

Horowitz, R. (Ed.) (in press). Talk about text: Developing understanding about the world through talk and text. Newark, DE: International Reading Association.

Idol-Maestas, L. (1985). Getting ready to read: Guided probing for poor comprehenders. Learning Disability Quarterly, 8(4), 243–254.

Jenkins, J. J. (1976). Four points to remember: A tetrahedral model of memory experiments. In L. S. Cermak & F. I. M. Craik (Eds.), Levels of processing in human memory. Hillsdale, NJ: Erlbaum.

Jenkins, J. R., Fuchs, L. S., Espin, C., van den Broek, P., & Deno, S. L. (2000, February). Effects of task format and performance dimension on word reading measures: Criterion validity, sensitivity to impairment, and context facilitation. Paper presented at Pacific Coast Research Conference, San Diego, CA.

Jiménez, R. T., García, G. E., & Pearson, P. D. (1996). The reading strategies of bilingual Latina/o students who are successful English readers: Opportunities and obstacles. Reading Research Quarterly, 31(1), 90–112.

Johnson-Laird, P. N. (1983). Mental models. Cambridge, MA: Harvard University Press.

Joyce, B., & Showers, B. (1996). Staff development as a comprehensive service organization. Journal of Staff Development, 17(1), 2–6.

Juel, C., Griffith, P. L., & Gough, P. B. (1986). Acquisition of literacy: A longitudinal study of children in first and second grade. Journal of Educational Psychology, 78, 243–255.

Just, M. A., & Carpenter, P. A. (1987). The psychology of reading and language comprehension. Needham Heights, MA: Allyn & Bacon.

Just, M. A., & Carpenter, P. A. (1992). A capacity theory of comprehension: Individual differences in working memory. Psychological Review, 99, 122–149.

Kamil, M. L., Intrator, S. M., & Kim, H. S. (2000). The effects of other technologies on literacy and literacy learning. In M. L. Kamil, P. B. Mosenthal, P. D. Pearson, & R. Barr (Eds.), Handbook of Reading Research: Volume III (pp. 771–788). Mahwah, NJ: Erlbaum.

Kamil, M. L., Mosenthal, P. B., Pearson, P. D., & Barr, R. (Eds.) (2000). Handbook of Reading Research. Mahwah, NJ: Erlbaum.

Keeny, T. J., Cannizzo, S. R., & Flavell, J. H. (1967). Spontaneous and induced verbal rehearsal in a recall task. Child Development, 38(4), 953–966.

Kemper, S., Jackson, J. D., Cheung, H., & Anagnopoulos, C. A. (1993). Enhancing older adults' reading comprehension. Discourse Processes, 15, 405–428.

Kintsch, W. (1974). The representation of meaning in memory. Hillsdale, NJ: Erlbaum.

Kintsch, W. (1998). Comprehension: A paradigm for cognition. New York: Cambridge University Press.

Klare, G. (1974–75). Assessing readability. Reading Research Quarterly, 10, 62–102.

Klare, G. (1976). A second look at the validity of readability formulas. Journal of Reading Behavior, 8(2), 129–152.

Kozma, R. B. (1991). Learning with media. Review of Educational Research, 61(2), 179–211.

Kuhn, M., & Stahl, S. (1998). Teaching children to learn word meanings from context: A synthesis and some questions. Journal of Literacy Research, 30, 119–138.

LaBerge, D., & Samuels, S. J. (1974). Toward a theory of automatic information processing in reading. Cognitive Psychology, 6, 293–323.

Labov, W. (1982). Objectivity and commitment in linguistic science. The case of the Black English trial in Ann Arbor. Language in Society, 11, 165–201.

Langer, J. A. (1984). Examining background knowledge and text comprehension. Reading Research Quarterly, 19, 468–481.

Lanier, J. E., & Little, J. W. (1986). Research on teacher education. In M. Wittrock (Ed.), Handbook of research on teaching (3rd ed., pp. 527–569). New York: Macmillan.

Lapp, D., Flood, J., & Ranck-Buhr, W. (1995). Using multiple text formats to explore scientific phenomena in middle school classrooms. Reading & Writing Quarterly: Overcoming Learning Difficulties, 11(2), 173–186.

Laufer, B., & Nation, P. (1999). A vocabulary-size test of controlled productive ability. Language Testing, 16(1), 33–51.

Laufer, B., & Sim, D. D. (1985). Measuring and explaining the reading threshold needed for English for academic purposes texts. Foreign Language Annals, 18(5), 405–411.

Lawless, K. A., & Kulikowich, J. M. (1996). Understanding hypertext navigation through cluster analysis. Journal of Educational Computing Research, 14(4), 385–399.

Lee, V. E. (2000). Using hierarchical linear modeling to study social contexts: The case of school effects. Educational Psychologist, 35(2), 125–141.

Lenhart, A., Rainie, L., & Lewis, O. (2001, June 20). Teenage life online. Available at www.pewinternet.org/reports/toc.asp?Report=36.

Leu, D. J. (1994, June). Designing hypermedia to connect reading and writing through children's literature. In Recreating the revolution. Proceedings of the annual National Educational Computing Conference. Boston, MA.

Levy, B. A., Abello, B., & Lysynchuk, L. (1977). Transfer from word training to reading in context: Gains in reading fluency and comprehension. Learning Disability Quarterly, 20, 173–188.

Liberman, I. Y. (1983). A language-oriented view of reading and its disabilities. In H. Myklebust (Ed.), Progress in learning disabilities (Vol. 5, pp. 81–101). New York: Grune & Stratton.

Lorch, R. F., & van den Broek, P. (1997). Understanding reading comprehension: Current and future contributions of Cognitive Science. Contemporary Educational Psychology, 22, 213–246.

Luke, A., & Elkins, J. (1998). Reinventing literacy in "New Times." Journal of Adolescent & Adult Literacy, 42, 4–7.

MacNamara, D., Kintsch, E., Songer, N. B., & Kintsch, W. (1996). Are good texts always better? Interactions of text coherence, background knowledge, and levels of understanding in learning from text. Cognition and Instruction, 14, 1–43.

Mandler, J. M. (1984). Stories, scripts, and scenes: Aspects of schema theory. Hillsdale, NJ: Erlbaum.

Mandler, J. M., & Johnson, N. S. (1977). Remembrance of things parsed: Story structure and recall. Cognitive Psychology, 9, 111–151.

Mannes, S. M., & Kintsch, W. (1987). Knowledge organization and text organization. Cognition and Instruction, 4, 91–115.

Mathes, P. G., & Fuchs, L. S. (1993). Peer-mediated reading instruction in special education resource rooms. Learning Disabilities Research and Practice, 8(4), 233–243.

Mayer, R. E. (1992). Knowledge and thought: Mental models that support scientific reasoning. In R. A. Duschl & R. J. Hamilton (Eds.), Philosophy of science, cognitive psychology, and educational theory and practice (pp. 226–243). Albany, NY: State University of New York Press.

Mayer, R. E. (1997). Multimedia learning: Are we asking the right questions? Educational Psychologist, 32(1), 1–19.

Mayer, R. E., & Moreno, R. (1998). A split-attention effect in multimedia learning: Evidence for dual processing systems in working memory. Journal of Educational Psychology, 90, 312–320.

Mayer, R. E., & Sims, V. K. (1994). For whom is a picture worth a thousand words? Extensions of a dual-coding theory of multimedia learning. Journal of Educational Psychology, 86(3), 389–401.

McDermott, R., & Varenne, H. (1995). Culture as disability. Anthropology & Education Quarterly, 26, 324–348.

McKeown, M. G. (1993). Creating effective definitions for young word learners. Reading Research Quarterly, 28(1), 16–31.

McKeown, M. G., Beck, I. L., Omanson, R. C., & Pople, M. T. (1985). Some effects of the nature and frequency of vocabulary instruction on the knowledge and use of words. Reading Research Quarterly, 20(5), 522–535.

Meichenbaum, D., & Biemiller, A. (1998). Nurturing independent learners: Helping students take charge of their learning. Cambridge, MA: Brookline.

Meyer, B. J. F., Brandt, D. M., & Bluth, G. J. (1980). Use of top-level structure in text: Key for reading comprehension of ninth-grade students. Reading Research Quarterly, 16, 72–103.

Meyer, B. J. F., & Freedle, R. O. (1984). Effects of discourse type on recall. American Educational Research Journal, 21(1), 121–143.

Meyer, M. S., & Felton, R. H. (1999). Repeated reading to enhance fluency: Old approaches and new directions. Annals of Dyslexia, 49, 283–306.

Mitchell, D. C. (1994). Sentence parsing. In M. A. Gernsbacher (Ed.), Handbook of psycholinguistics (pp. 375–409). San Diego, CA: Academic Press.

Moje, E. B., Young, J. P., Readence, J. E., & Moore, D. W. (2000). Reinventing adolescent literacy for new times: Perennial and millennial issues. Journal of Adolescent & Adult Literacy, 43, 400–410.

Moore, D. W., Alvermann, D. E., & Hinchman, K. A. (Eds.). (2000). Struggling adolescent readers. Newark, DE: International Reading Association.

Morrison, T. G., Jacobs, J. S., & Swinyard, W. (1999). Do teachers who read personally use recommended literacy practices in their classrooms? Reading Research and Instruction, 38(2), 81–100.

Morrow, L. M., & Gambrell, L. B. (2001). Literature-based instruction in the early years. In S. B. Neuman & D. K. Dickinson (Eds.), Handbook of early literacy research (pp. 348–360). New York: The Guilford Press.

Muniz-Swicegood, M. (1994). The effects of metacognitive reading strategy training on the reading performance and fluent reading analysis strategies of third grade bilingual students. Bilingual Research Journal, 18, 83–97.

Muter, V., & Diethelm, K. (2001). The contribution of phonological skills and letter knowledge to early reading development in a multilingual population. Language Learning, 51(2), 187–219.

Nagy, W., García, G. E., Durgunoglu, A., & Hancin-Bhatt, B. (1993). Spanish-English bilingual students' use of cognates in English reading. Journal of Reading Behavior, 25(3), 241–259.

Nagy, W. E., McClure, E. F., & Montserrat, M. (1997). Linguistic transfer and the use of context by Spanish-English bilinguals. Applied Psycholinguistics, 18(4), 431–452.

Nagy, W. E., & Scott, J. A. (1990). Word schemas: Expectations about the form and meaning of new words. Cognition & Instruction, 7(2), 105–127.

Nagy, W. E., & Scott, J. A. (2000). Vocabulary processes. In M. L. Kamil, P. B. Mosenthal, P. D. Pearson, & R. Barr (Eds.), Handbook of reading research: Volume III (pp. 269–284). Mahwah, NJ: Erlbaum.

Nathan, M. J., Kintsch, W., & Young, E. (1992). A theory of word algebra problem-comprehension and its implications for the design of the learning environments. Cognition and Instruction, 9, 329–389.

Nation, P. (1989). A system of tasks for language learning. In A. Sarinee (Ed.), Language teaching methodology for the nineties. Selected papers from the Southeast Asian Ministers of Education Organization (SEAMEO) Regional Language Centre Seminar (1989). Anthology Series 24.

National Reading Panel (NRP). (2000). Teaching children to read: An evidence-based assessment of the scientific research literature on reading and its implications for reading instruction. Washington, DC: National Institute of Child Health and Human Development.

Nelson, J. R., Smith, D. J., & Dodd, J. M. (1992). The effects of teaching a summary skills strategy to students identified as learning disabled on their comprehension of science text. Education & Treatment of Children, 15(3), 228–243.

Neuman, S. B. (1999). Books make a difference: A study of access to literacy. Reading Research Quarterly, 34, 281–312.

Neuman, S. B., & Dickinson, D. K. (Eds.). (2001). Handbook of early literacy research. Mahwah, NJ: Erlbaum.

Neuman, S. B., & Roskos, K. (1990). The influence of literacy-enriched play settings on preschoolers' engagement with written language. In J. Zutell & S. McCormick (Eds.), Literacy theory and research: analyses from multiple perspectives (pp. 179–187). Chicago: National Reading Conference.

Neuman, S. B., & Roskos, K. (1997). Literacy knowledge in practice: Contexts of participation for young writers and readers. Reading Research Quarterly, 32, 10–33.

Nevitt, J., & Hancock, G. R. (2000). Improving the root mean square error of approximation for nonnormal conditions in structural equation modeling. Journal of Experimental Education, 68(3), 251–268.

Norman, D. A., & Bobrow, D. G. (1975). On data-limited and resource-limited processes. Cognitive Psychology, 7(1), 44–64.

Nystrand, M. (1986). The structure of written communication: Studies in reciprocity between readers and writers. Norwood, NJ: Ablex.

Nystrand, M. (1990). High school English students in low-achieving classes: What helps? Newsletter: National Center for Effective Secondary Schools, 5, 7–8, 11.

O'Brien, D. G. (1998). Multiple literacies in a high-school program for "at-risk" adolescents. In D. E. Alvermann, K. A. Hinchman, D. W. Moore, S. F. Phelps, & D. R. Waff (Eds.), Reconceptualizing the literacies in adolescents' lives (pp. 27–49). Mahwah, NJ: Erlbaum.

O'Brien, D. G. (2001). "At-risk" adolescents: Redefining competence through the multiliteracies of intermediality, visual arts, and representation. Reading Online, 4(11). Available at www.readingonline.org/newliteracies/lit_index.asp?

Office of Science and Technology Policy. (1998). Investing in our future: A national research initiative for America's children for the 21st century. Washington, DC: The White House.

Oldfather, P., & McLaughlin, H. J. (1993). Gaining and losing voice: A longitudinal study of students' continuing impulse to learn across elementary and middle school contexts. Research in Middle Level Education, 3, 1–25.

Olson, D. R. (1977). From utterance to text: The bias of language in speech and writing. Harvard Educational Review, 42(3), 257–281.

Olson, D. R. (1994). The world on paper. Cambridge: Cambridge University Press.

Otero, J., Leon, J. A., & Graesser, A. C. (Eds.). (in press). Scientific text comprehension. Mahwah, NJ: Erlbaum.

Padrón, Y. (1994). Comparing reading instruction in Hispanic/limited English-proficient schools and other inner-city schools. Bilingual Research Journal, 18, 49–66.

Paivio, A. (1971). Imagery and verbal processes. New York: Holt.

Paivio, A. (1986). Mental representations: A dual coding approach. New York: Oxford University Press.

Paivio, A., & Begg, I. (1971). Imagery and comprehension latencies as a function of sentence concreteness and structure. Perception and Psychophysics, 10, 408–412.

Pajares, F. (1996). Self-efficacy beliefs in academic settings. Review of Educational Research, 66, 543–578.

Palincsar, A. S., & Brown, A. (1984). Reciprocal teaching of comprehension-fostering and comprehension-monitoring activities. Cognition and Instruction, 1, 117–175.

Pappas, C. C., & Barry, A. (1997). Scaffolding urban students' initiations: Transactions in reading information books in the read-aloud curriculum genre. In N. J. Karolides (Ed.), Reader response in elementary classrooms: Quest and discovery (pp. 215–236). Hillsdale, NJ: Erlbaum.

Pearson, P. D. (2001). Life in the radical middle: A personal apology for a balanced view of reading. In R. Flippo (Ed.), Reading researchers in search of common ground (pp. 78–83). Newark, DE: International Reading Association.

Pearson, P. D., & Fielding, L. (1991). Comprehension instruction. In R. Barr, M. L. Kamil, P. Mosenthal, & P. D. Pearson (Eds.), Handbook of reading research: Volume II (pp. 815–860). New York: Longman.

Pedhazur, E. J., & Schmelkin, L. P. (1991). Measurement, design, and analysis: An integrated approach. Hillsdale, NJ: Erlbaum.

Perfetti, C. A. (1985). Reading ability. New York: Oxford Press.

Perfetti, C. A. (1994). Psycholinguistics and reading ability. In M. A. Gernsbacher (Ed.), Handbook of psycholinguistics (pp. 849–894). San Diego, CA: Academic Press.

Pinnell, G. S., Lyons, C. A., DeFord, D., & Bryk, A. S. (1994). Comparing instructional models for the literacy education of high-risk first graders. Reading Research Quarterly, 29(1), 8–39.

Pinnell, G. S., Pikulski, J. J., Wixson, K. K., Campbell, J. R., Gough, P. B., & Beatty, A. S. (1995). Listening to children read aloud. Washington, DC: Office of Educational Research and Improvement, U.S. Department of Education.

Plass, J. L., Chun, D. M., Mayer, R. E., & Leutner, D. (1998). Supporting visual and verbal learning preferences in a second-language multimedia learning environment. Journal of Educational Psychology, 90(1), 25–36.

Posner, M. I., & Snyder, C. R. R. (1975). Attention and cognitive control. In R. L. Solso (Ed.), Information processing and cognition: The Loyola symposium (pp. 55–85). Hillsdale, NJ: Erlbaum.

Pressley, M. (1977). Imagery and children's learning: Putting the picture in developmental perspective. Review of Educational Research, 47, 585–622.

Pressley, M. (2000). What should comprehension instruction be the instruction of? In M. Kamil, P. Mosenthal, P. D. Pearson, & R. Barr (Eds.), Handbook of reading research, Volume III (pp. 545–562). Mahwah, NJ: Erlbaum

Pressley, M., & Afflerbach, P. (1995). Verbal protocols of reading: The nature of constructively responsive reading. Hillsdale, NJ: Erlbaum.

Pressley, M., & Miller, G. E. (1987). Effects of illustrations on children's listening comprehension and oral prose memory. In D. M. Willows & H. A. Houghton (Eds.), The psychology of illustration: Volume 1. Basic research (pp. 87–114). New York: Springer-Verlag.

Pressley, M., Wharton-McDonald, R., Allington, R., Block, C. C., Morrow, L., Tracey, D., Baker, K., Brooks, G., Cronin, J., Nelson, E., & Woo, D. (2001). A study of effective first-grade literacy instruction. Scientific Studies of Reading, 5(1), 35–58.

Ramirez, J. D., Yuen, S. D., & Ramey, D. R. (1991). Executive summary: Final report: Longitudinal study of structured English immersion strategy, early-exit and late-exit transitional bilingual education programs for language minority children. San Mateo, CA: Aguirre International.

Rashotte, C., & Torgesen, J. (1985). Repeated reading and reading fluency in learning disabled children. Reading Research Quarterly, 20, 180–188.

Rasinski, T. V. (1990). Effects of repeated reading and listening-while-reading on reading fluency. Journal of Educational Research, 83(3), 147–150.

Recht, D. R., & Leslie, L. (1988). Effect of prior knowledge on good and poor readers' memory of text. Journal of Educational Psychology, 80, 16–20.

Reeve, J., Bolt, E., & Cai, Y. (1999). Autonomy-supportive teachers: How they teach and motivate students. Journal of Educational Psychology, 91(3), 537–548.

Reichle, E. D., Carpenter, P. A., & Just, M. A. (2000). The neural bases of strategy and skill in sentence-picture verification. Cognitive Psychology, 40(4), 261–295.

Reutzel, D. R., & Hollingsworth, P. M. (1993). Effects of fluency training on second graders' reading comprehension. Journal of Educational Research, 86(6), 325–331.

Reynolds, R. E., Taylor, M. A., Steffensen, M. S., Shirey, L. L., & Anderson, R. C. (1982). Cultural schemata and reading comprehension. Reading Research Quarterly, 17, 353–366.

Ringel, B. A., & Springer, C. J. (1980). On knowing how well one is remembering: The persistence of strategy use during transfer. Journal of Experimental Child Psychology, 29(2), 322–333.

Roberts, B. (1992). The evolution of the young child's concept of "word" as a unit of spoken and written language. Reading Research Quarterly, 27(2), 124–138.

Rosenblatt, L. M. (1994). The reader, the text, the poem: The transactional theory of the literary work. Carbondale, IL: Southern Illinois University Press. Original work published in 1978.

Rosenshine, B., & Meister, C. (1994). Reciprocal teaching: A review of the research. Review of Educational Research, 64, 479–530.

Roskos, K., & Neuman, S. B. (2001). Environment and its influences for early literacy teaching and learning. In S. B. Neuman & D. K. Dickinson (Eds.), Handbook of early literacy research (pp. 281–292). Mahwah, NJ: Erlbaum.

Scarborough, H. S. (2001). Connecting early language and later reading (dis)abilities: Evidence, theory, and practice. In S. B. Neuman & D. K. Dickinson (Eds.) Handbook of early literacy research (pp. 97–110). New York: The Guilford Press.

Schafer, W. D. (1999). An overview of meta-analysis. Measurement and Evaluation in Counseling and Development, 32(1), 43–61.

Schank, R. C. (1999). Dynamic memory revisited. Cambridge: Cambridge University Press.

Schiefele, U. (1999). Interest and learning from text. Scientific Studies of Reading, 3(3), 257–279.

Schneider, W., Koerkel, J., & Weinert, F. E. (1989). Domain-specific knowledge and memory performance: A comparison of high- and low-aptitude children. Journal of Educational Psychology, 81(3), 306–312.

Schraw, G., & Bruning, R. (1996). Readers' implicit models of reading. Reading Research Quarterly, 31(3), 290–305.

Schreiber, P. A. (1980). On the acquisition of reading fluency. Journal of Reading Behavior, 12, 177–186.

Schreiber, P. A. (1987). Prosody and structure in children's syntactic processing. In R. Horowitz & S. J. Samuels (Eds.), Comprehending oral and written language. New York: Academic Press.

Schumaker, J. B., Deshler, D. D., Alley, G. R., Varner, M. M., Clark, F. L., & Nolan, S. (1982). Error monitoring: A learning strategy for improving adolescent academic performance. In W. M. Cruickshank & J. W. Lerner (Eds.), Coming of age: Vol. 3. The Best of ACLD (pp. 170–183). Syracuse, NY: Syracuse University Press.

Schunk, D. H., & Rice, J. M. (1993). Strategy fading and progress feedback: Effects on self-efficacy and comprehension among students receiving remedial reading services. Journal of Special Education, 27, 257–276.

Scott, J. A., & Nagy, W. E. (1997). Understanding the definitions of unfamiliar verbs. Reading Research Quarterly, 32(2), 184–200.

Semali, L., & Pailliotet, A. W. (1999). Intermediality: The teachers' handbook of critical media literacy. Boulder, CO: Westview.

Shake, M. C. (1986). Teacher interruptions during oral reading instruction: Self-monitoring as an impetus for change in corrective feedback. Remedial and Special Education (RASE), 7(5), 18–24.

Shaywitz, B. A., Fletcher, J. M., & Shaywitz, S. E. (1995). Defining and classifying learning disabilities and attention-deficit/hyperactivity disorder. Journal of Child Neurology, 10 (Suppl.), S50–S57.

Shaywitz, B. A., Pugh, K. R., Jenner, A. R., Fulbright, R. K., Fletcher, J. M., Gore, J. C., & Shaywitz, S. E. (2000). The neurobiology of reading and reading disability (dyslexia). In M. L. Kamil, P. B. Mosenthal, P. D. Pearson, & R. Barr (Eds.), Handbook of reading research: Volume III (pp. 229–249). Mahwah, NJ: Erlbaum.

Shin, E. C., Schallert, D. L., & Savenye, W. C. (1994). Effects of learner control, advisement, and prior knowledge on young students' learning in a hypertext environment. Educational Technology Research & Development, 42(1), 33–46.

Shulman, L. S. (1986). Those who understand: Knowledge growth in teaching. Educational Researcher, 15(2), 4–14.

Siegel, L. S. (1988). Evidence that IQ scores are irrelevant to the definition and analysis of reading disability. Canadian Journal of Psychology, 42, 201–215.

Sikula, J. (1996). Handbook of research on teacher education (2nd ed.). New York: Macmillan.

Simmons, D. C., Fuchs, D., Fuchs, L. S., Hodge, J. P., & Mathes, P. G. (1994). Importance of instructional complexity and role reciprocity to classwide peer tutoring. Learning Disabilities Research and Practice, 9(4), 203–212.

Singer, M., Harkness, D., & Moore, S. (in press). Constructing inferences in expository text comprehension. Discourse Processes.

Skinner, E. A., Wellborn, J. G., & Connell, J. P. (1990). What it takes to do well in school and whether I've got it: A process model of perceived control and children's engagement and achievement in school. Journal of Educational Psychology, 82(1), 22–32.

Slavin, R. E., Madden, N. A., Karweit, N. I., Dolan, L., & Wasik, B. A. (1992). Success for all: A relentless approach to prevention and early intervention in elementary schools. Arlington, VA: Educational Research Service.

Snow, C. E. (1993). Families as social contexts for literacy development. New Directions for Child Development, 61, 11–24.

Snow, C. E., Barnes, W., Chandler, J., Goodman, I., & Hemphill, L. (1991). Unfulfilled expectations: Home and school influences on literacy. Cambridge, MA: Harvard.

Snow, C. E., Burns, M. S., & Griffin, P. (Eds.) (1998). Preventing reading difficulties in young children. Washington, DC: National Academy Press.

Sonnenschein, S., Baker, L., Serpell, R., Scher, D., Truitt, V. G., & Munsterman, K. (1997). Parental beliefs about ways to help children learn to read: The impact of an entertainment or a skills perspective. Early Child Development & Care, 127–128, 111–118.

Spiro, R. J., & Myers, A. (1984). Individual differences and underlying cognitive processes in reading. In P. Pearson, R. Barr, M. Kamil, & P. Mosenthal, Handbook of reading research (pp. 471–501). New York: Longman.

Stahl, S. A., & Fairbanks, M. M. (1986). The effects of vocabulary instruction: A model-based meta-analysis. Review of Educational Research, 56(1), 72–110.

Stahl, S. A., Richek, M. A., & Vandevier, R. J. (1991). Learning meaning vocabulary through listening: A sixth-grade replication. National Reading Conference Yearbook, 40, 185–192.

Stanovich, K. E. (1986). Matthew effects in reading: Some consequences of individual differences in the acquisition of literacy. Reading Research Quarterly, 16, 32–71.

Stanovitch, K. E. (1991). Word recognition: Changing perspectives. In R. Barr, M. Kamil, P. Mosenthal, & P. D. Pearson (Eds.), Handbook of reading research: Volume II (pp. 418–452). New York: Longman.

Stanovich, K. E., & Cunningham, A. E. (1992). Studying the consequences of literacy within a literate society: The cognitive correlates of print exposure. Memory & Cognition, 20, 51–68.

Stanovich, K. E., & Siegel, L. S. (1994). Phenotypic performance profile of children with reading disabilities: A regression-based test of the phonological-core variable-difference model. Journal of Educational Psychology, 86(1), 24–53.

Stein, N. L., & Glenn, C. (1979). An analysis of story comprehension in elementary school children. In R. Freedle (Ed.), New directions in discourse processing: Vol. 2. Advances in discourse processing (pp. 53–120). Norwood, NJ: Ablex.

Stein, N. L., & Trabasso, T. (1981). What's in a story: Critical issues in comprehension and instruction. In R. Glaser (Ed.), Advances in the psychology of instruction: Vol. 2. Hillsdale, NJ: Erlbaum.

Sticht, T. G., & James, J. H. (1984). Listening and reading. In P. D. Pearson, R. Barr, M. Kamil, & P. Mosenthal (Eds.), Handbook of reading research (pp. 292–317). New York: Longman.

Stigler, J. W., Gallimore, R., & Hiebert, J. (2000). Using video surveys to compare classrooms and teaching across cultures: Examples and lessons from the TIMSS video studies. Educational Psychologist, 35(2), 87–100.

Stigler, J. W., Gonzales, P., Kawanaka, T., Knoll, S., & Serrano, A. (1999). The TIMSS videotape classroom study: Methods and findings from an exploratory research project on eighth-grade mathematics instruction in Germany, Japan, and the United States. Education Statistics Quarterly, 1(2), 109–112.

Strickland, D. S. (2001). Early intervention for African American children considered to be at risk. In S. B. Neuman & D. K. Dickinson (Eds.), Handbook of early literacy research (pp. 323–332). New York: Guilford Press.

Swanson, H. L., Kozleski, E., & Stegink, P. (1987). Disabled readers' processing of prose: Do any processes change because of intervention? Psychology in the Schools, 24(4), 378–384.

Swanson, H. L., & Siegel, L. (in press). Learning disabilities as a working memory deficit. Issues in Education: Contributions from Educational Psychology.

Sweet, A. P., Guthrie, J. T., & Ng, M. M. (1998). Teacher perceptions and student motivation. Journal of Educational Psychology, 90(2), 210–223.

Sykes, G. (1999). Teacher and student learning: Strengthening their connection. In L. Darling-Hammond & G. Sykes (Eds.), Teaching as the learning profession: Handbook of policy and practice (pp. 151–180). San Francisco: Jossey-Bass.

Tabors, P. O., & Snow, C. E. (2001). Young bilingual children and early literacy development. In S. B. Neuman & D. K. Dickinson (Eds.), Handbook of early literacy research (pp. 159–178). New York: Guilford Press.

Tan, A., & Nicholson, T. (1997). Flash cards revisited: Training poor readers to read words faster improves their comprehension of text. Journal of Educational Psychology, 89, 276–288.

Taylor, B. M. (1985). Improving middle-grade students' reading and writing of expository text. Journal of Educational Research, 79(2), 119–125.

Taylor, B. M., Pearson, P. D., Clark, K. F., & Walpole, S. (1999). Effective schools/accomplished teachers. Reading Teacher, 53(2), 156–159.

Tharp, R. G., & Gallimore, R. (1988). Rousing minds to life: Teaching, learning, and schooling in social context. Cambridge: Cambridge University Press.

Tierney, R. J., & Cunningham, J. W. (1984). Research on teaching reading comprehension. In P. D. Pearson, R. Barr, M. L. Kamil, & P. Mosenthal (Eds.), Handbook of reading research (pp. 609–656). New York: Longman.

Tinkham, T. (1993). The effect of semantic clustering on the learning of second language vocabulary. System, 21(3), 371–380.

Torgesen, J. K. (2000). Individual differences in response to early interventions in reading: The lingering problem of treatment resisters. Learning Disabilities Research and Practice, 15(1), 55–64.

Torgesen, J., Rashotte, C., & Alexander, A. (in press). The prevention and remediation of reading fluency problems. In M. Wolf (Ed.), Dyslexia, fluency, and the brain. Timonium. MD: York Press.

Torgesen, J. K., Wagner, R. K., & Rashotte, C. A. (1999). Preventing reading failure in young children with phonological processing disabilities: Group and individual responses to instruction. Journal of Educational Psychology, 91, 579–594.

Tunmer, W. E., Herriman, M. L., & Nesdale, A. R. (1988). Metalinguistic abilities and beginning reading. Reading Research Quarterly, 23, 134–158.

Turner, J. C. (1995). The influence of classroom contexts on young children's motivation for literacy. Reading Research Quarterly, 30(3), 410–441.

Turner, J. C., & Meyer, D. K. (2000). Studying and understanding the instructional contexts of classrooms: Using our past to forge our future. Educational Psychologist, 35(2), 69–85.

Valdés, G. (1996). Con respeto. Bridging the distances between culturally diverse families and schools. An ethnographic portrait. New York: Teachers College Press.

van Dijk, T., & Kintsch, W. (1983). Strategies of discourse comprehension. San Diego, CA: Academic Press.

Van Dongen, R., & Westby, C. E. (1986). Building the narrative mode of thought through children's literature. Topics in Language Disorders, 7(1), 70–83.

van Oostendorp, H., & Goldman, S. R. (Eds.). (1999). The construction of mental representations during reading. Mahwah, NJ: Erlbaum.

Vellutino, F. R. (1979). Dyslexia: Theory and research. Cambridge, MA: MIT Press.

Vellutino, F. R. (1987, March). Dyslexia. Scientific American, 34–41.

Vellutino, F. R. (in press). Working memory deficits and learning disabilities: Reactions to Swanson Siegel. Issues in Education: Contributions from Educational Psychology.

Vellutino, F. R., & Scanlon, D. M. (1985). Free recall of concrete and abstract words in poor and normal readers. Journal of Experimental Child Psychology, 39, 363–380.

Vellutino, F. R., & Scanlon, D. M. (2001). Emergent literacy skills, early instruction, and individual differences as determinants of difficulties in learning to read: The case for early intervention. In S. B. Neuman & D. K. Dickinson (Eds.), Handbook of early literacy research (pp. 295–321). New York: The Guilford Press.

Vellutino, F. R., & Scanlon, D. M. (in press). The interactive strategies approach to reading intervention. Contemporary Educational Psychology.

Vellutino, F. R, Scanlon, D. M., & Lyon, G. R. (2000). Differentiating between difficult to remediate and readily remediated poor readers: More evidence against the IQ Achievement discrepancy definition of reading disability. Journal of Learning Disabilities, 33(3), 223–238.

Vellutino, F. R., Scanlon, D. M., Sipay, E. R., Small, S. G., Pratt, A., Chen, R. & Denckla, M. B. (1996). Cognitive profiles of difficult to remediate and readily remediated poor readers: Early intervention as a vehicle for distinguishing between cognitive and experiential deficits as basic causes of specific reading disability. Journal of Educational Psychology, 88(4), 601–638.

Vellutino, F. R., Scanlon, D. M., Small, S. G., & Tanzman, M. S. (1991). The linguistic basis of reading ability: converting written to oral language. Text, 11, 99–133.

Vellutino, F. R., Scanlon, D. M., & Spearing, D. (1995). Semantic and phonological coding in poor and normal readers. Journal of Experimental Child Psychology, 59, 76–123.

Vellutino, F. R., Scanlon, D. M., & Tanzman, M. S. (1988). Lexical memory in poor and normal readers: Developmental differences in the use of category cues. Canadian Journal of Psychology, 42, 216–241.

Vellutino, F. R., Scanlon, D. M., & Tanzman, M. S. (1994). Components of reading ability: Issues and problems in operationalizing word identification, phonological coding, and orthographic coding. In G. R. Lyon (Ed.), Frames of reference for the assessment of learning disabilities: New views on measurement issues (pp. 279–329). Baltimore: Paul H. Brookes.

Venezky, R. L. (1998) An alternative perspective on Success for All. Advances in Educational Policy, 4, 145–165.

Vernon-Feagans, L., Hammer, C. S., Miccio, A., & Manlove, E. (2001). Early language and literacy skills in low-income African American and Hispanic children. In S. B. Neuman & D. K. Dickinson (Eds.), Handbook of early literacy research (pp. 192–210). New York: The Guilford Press.

Vygotsky, L. S. (1978). Mind in society: The development of higher psychological processes. Cambridge, MA: Harvard University Press.

Walker, C. H. (1987). Relative importance of domain knowledge and overall aptitude on acquisition of domain-related information. Cognition and Instruction, 4, 25–42.

Waring, R. (1997). The negative effects of learning words in semantic sets: A replication. System, 25(2), 261–274.

Watson, R. (2001). Literacy and oral language: Implications for early literacy acquisition. In S. B. Neuman & D. K. Dickinson (Eds.), Handbook of early literacy research (pp. 43–53). New York: The Guilford Press.

Watson, R., & Olson, D. R. (1987). From meaning to definition: A literature bias on the structure of word meaning. In R. Horowitz & J. Samuels (Eds.), Comprehending oral and written language (pp. 329–354). San Diego, CA: Academic Press.

Whipple, G. (Ed.). (1925). The twenty-fourth yearbook of the National Society for the Study of Education: Report of the National Committee on Reading. Bloomington, IL: Public School Publishing Company.

Whitehurst, G. J., & Lonigan, C. J. (1998). Child development and emergent literacy. Child Development, 69(3), 848–872.

Whitehurst, G. R., & Lonigan, C. J. (2001). Emergent Literacy: Development from prereaders to readers. In S. B. Neuman & D. K. Dickinson (Eds.), Handbook of early literacy research (pp. 11–29). New York: The Guilford Press.

Wiley, T. G. (1996). Language planning and policy. In S. L. McKay & N. H. Hornberger (Eds.), Sociolinguistics and language teaching. Cambridge: Cambridge University Press.

Williams, J. P. (1993). Comprehension of students with and without learning disabilities: Identification of narrative themes and idiosyncratic text representations. Journal of Educational Psychology, 85, 631–641.

Willis, A. I., & Harris, V. J. (2000). Political acts: Literacy learning and teaching. Reading Research Quarterly, 35 (1), 72–88.

Wolf, M., Bowers, P. G., & Biddle, K. (2000). Naming-speed processes, timing, and reading: A conceptual review. Journal of Learning Disabilities, 33, 387–407.

Wolf, M., & Katzir-Cohen, T. (2001). Reading fluency and its intervention. Scientific Studies of Reading, 5(3), 211–239.

Wong, B. Y. L., & Jones, W. (1982). Increasing metacomprehension in learning disabled and normally achieving students through self-questioning training. Learning Disability Quarterly, 5(3), 228–240.

Yekovich, F. R., Walker, C. H., Ogle, L. T., & Thompson, M. A. (1990). The influence of domain knowledge on inferencing in low-aptitude individuals. In A. C. Graesser & G. H. Bower (Eds.), The Psychology of Learning and Motivation , Vol. 25 (pp. 175–196). New York: Academic Press.

Zwaan, R. A., Langston, M. C., & Graesser, A. C. (1995). The construction of situation models in narrative comprehension: An event-indexing model. Psychological Science, 6, 292–297.

Zwaan, R. A., Magliano, J. P., & Graesser, A. C. (1995). Dimensions of situation model construction in narrative comprehension. Journal of Experimental Psychology: Learning, Memory, and Cognition, 21, 386–397.

Zwaan, R. A., & Radvansky, G. A. (1998). Situation models in language comprehension and memory. Psychological Bulletin, 123, 162–185.

CATHERINE SNOW (Chair) is the Henry Lee Shattuck Professor of Education at the Harvard Graduate School of Education. She received her Ph.D. in psychology from McGill University and worked for several years in the linguistics department of the University of Amsterdam. Her research interests include children's language development as influenced by interaction with adults in home and preschool settings, literacy development as related to language skills and as influenced by home and school factors, and issues related to the acquisition of English-language oral and literacy skills by language minority children. She has co-authored books on language development (e.g., *Pragmatic Development* with Anat Ninio) and on literacy development (e.g., *Unfulfilled Expectations: Home and School Influences on Literacy* with W. Barnes, J. Chandler, I. Goodman, and L. Hemphill) and has published widely on these topics in refereed journals and edited volumes. Dr. Snow's contributions to the education field include membership on the editorial boards of several journals, co-directorship for several years of the Child Language Data Exchange System, and editorship of *Applied Psycholinguistics*. She served as a board member at the Center for Applied Linguistics and a member of the National Research Council (NRC) Committee on Establishing a Research Agenda on Schooling for Language Minority Children. She chaired the National Research Council Committee on Preventing Reading Difficulties in Young Children, which produced a report that has been widely adopted as a basis for reforming reading instruction and professional development. She currently serves on the NRC's Council for the Behavioral and Social Sciences and Education and is past president of the American Educational Research Association. A member of the National Academy of Education, Dr. Snow has held visiting appointments at the University of Cambridge, England; Universidad Autonoma, Madrid; and The Institute of Advanced Studies at Hebrew University, Jerusalem. She has guest taught at Universidad Central de Caracas, El Colegio de Mexico, Odense University in Denmark, and several institutions in The Netherlands.

DONNA E. ALVERMANN is a research professor of reading education at the University of Georgia and a professor of reading education. Her research focuses on adolescent literacy. Currently, she is completing data collection on a Spencer Foundation major grant that includes a 15-week intervention aimed at teaching media literacy to a group of 30 middle and high school students. From 1992 to 1997, Dr. Alvermann co-directed the National Reading Research Center and conducted three long-term studies of adolescents' perceptions of reading and learning from text-based discussions. At the start of that research program, the literature on adolescent literacy development contained very little information on what it means to be a motivated, or even disinterested, reader from an adolescent's perspective. This perspective is important because teachers generally tend to act more readily on students' perceptions than they do on the research and theorizing of those in academe. Dr. Alvermann is past president of the National Reading Conference and served as co-chair of the International Reading Association's Commission on Adolescent Literacy from 1997 to 2000. Currently, she is a member of the Board of Directors of the College Reading Association, the Chair of the Board of Directors of the American Reading Forum, and a co-editor of the *Journal of Literacy Research*. In 1997, she was awarded the Oscar S. Causey Award for Outstanding Contributions to Reading Research.

JANICE DOLE is currently an associate professor of reading education at the University of Utah. After several years as an elementary teacher, Dr. Dole completed her M.A. and Ph.D. at the University of Colorado. Subsequently, she held positions at the University of Denver, the Center for the Study of Reading at the University of Illinois at Urbana-Champaign, and Michigan State University. Dr. Dole has written for many different audiences, including teachers and administrators (*Elementary School Journal, Journal of Reading*) and reading researchers and other educational researchers (*Reading Research Quarterly, Review of Educational Research*). She is currently on the Reading Development Panel for the National Assessment of Educational Progress and has worked for the research and development section of the American Federation for Teachers for the past five years. Three years ago, she took a leave of absence from the University of Utah to work for the Utah State Office of Education. There she served as the director of the Governor's Literacy Initiative for Utah. In this capacity, she directed a $250,000 professional development project for the state. In addition, she led the state in receiving a $7 million grant for the Reading Excellence Act from the U.S. Department of Education. Her current research interests include comprehension instruction at the K–3 level and reading professional development for K–3 teachers in at-risk schools.

JACK M. FLETCHER, Ph.D., is a professor in the Department of Pediatrics at the University of Texas-Houston Health Science Center and associate director of the Center for Academic and Reading Skills. During the past 20 years, Dr. Fletcher, a child neuropsychologist, has completed research on many aspects of the development of reading, language, and other cognitive skills in children. He has worked extensively on issues related to learning and attention problems, including definition and classification, neurobiological correlates, and, most recently, intervention. He collaborates on several grants on reading and attention funded by the National Institute of Child Health and Human Development, the U.S. Department of Education, and the National Science Foundation under the Interagency Educational Research Initiative. Dr. Fletcher is also principal investigator or co–principal investigator on National Institutes of Health–funded research projects involving children with brain injuries, including a program project on spina bifida and other projects involving children with traumatic brain injury. Dr. Fletcher served on and chaired the NICHD Mental Retardation/Developmental Disabilities study section and is a former member of the NICHD Maternal and Child Health study section. He chaired a committee on children with persistent reading disability for the Houston Independent School District (HISD) and served on a task force on reading for HISD that produced a report widely cited within the state of Texas as a model for enhancing reading instruction in elementary school children. Dr. Fletcher has received several service awards from local school districts. He is part of a large consortium of investigators from the University of Houston, University of Texas-Houston, University of Texas-Austin, and California State University-Long Beach who applied for a program project grant involving the development of literacy skills in Spanish-speaking and bilingual children under the recent NICHD/Department of Education Bilingual Research Initiative.

GEORGIA EARNEST GARCÍA is an associate professor and Associate Head of the Department of Curriculum and Instruction at the University of Illinois at Urbana-Champaign. She holds a zero-time appointment in the Department of Educational Policy Studies and is a faculty affiliate with the Latina/Latinos Studies Program. A former Title VII Bilingual Education Fellow, she obtained her Ph.D. in Education from the University of Illinois in 1988. She currently teaches courses in reading, bilingual education/ESL, sociolinguistics, and multicultural education. Her research focuses on the literacy development, instruction, and assessment of students from culturally, linguistically, and economically diverse backgrounds, with much of her current research focusing on bilingual reading. She has published her work in the *American Educational Research Journal, Anthropology and Education Quarterly, Review of Research in Education, Reading Research Quarterly,* and the *Journal of Literacy Research.* She was named a College of Education Distinguished Scholar in 1997 and was awarded the Faculty Award for Excellence in Graduate Teaching, Advising, and Research by the Council of Graduate Students in Education in 1993. Dr. García was a senior research scientist at the Center for the Study of Reading for six years. She currently serves on the Board of Directors for the National Reading Conference.

IRENE W. GASKINS, a school administrator and founder of Benchmark School, is, above all, a teacher and instructional leader. Throughout her career she has been involved in many aspects of reading education. Dr. Gaskins taught in the public schools in Virginia and Pennsylvania. In 1965, she received her master's degree in Reading Education from the University of Pennsylvania and became a research assistant in the reading clinic there. As a research assistant, she tracked the characteristics and progress of struggling readers in Penn's dyslexia study. This experience piqued her interest in bright children who have great difficulty learning to read. Her dissertation research addressed this topic. Stints as a district reading consultant, college teacher, and consultant with a publishing company were followed by Dr. Gaskins' receiving her doctorate in educational psychology in 1970 from the University of Pennsylvania. Sparked by her interest in children who have profound difficulties in learning to read, Dr. Gaskins founded Benchmark School in Media, Pennsylvania, in 1970. Dr. Gaskins designed Benchmark to be a special school for helping struggling readers, but she also wanted it to be a laboratory for designing instruction that works for all students. Collaborating with her energetic and dedicated faculty, as well as with major consultants from around the country, Dr. Gaskins has worked on such significant problems as designing word-recognition instruction that works for students who previously made little progress in this area, improving reading performance by increasing students' awareness and control of cognitive styles and other personal factors that affect reading, and designing programs that teach strategies for understanding and learning from texts. During 1988 to 1994, the strategies research at Benchmark was funded by the James S. McDonnell Foundation, and Benchmark was the foundation's national demonstration school. The part of her job that Dr. Gaskins likes most is being the teacher, or co-teacher, who pilots and fine-tunes the new programs being developed at Benchmark. The results of this work have been published in such journals as *The Reading Teacher, Reading Research Quarterly*, the *Journal of Reading Behavior, Language Arts, Elementary School Journal, Remedial and Special Education*, and the *Journal of Learning Disabilities*.

THOMAS K. GLENNAN, JR., obtained his Ph.D. in economics at Stanford University. He is a senior advisor for education policy in the Washington office of RAND. His research at RAND has spanned a wide variety of policy-planning issues in such diverse areas as education, manpower training, energy, environmental enforcement, demonstration program management in health and human services, and military research and development. Through 1997, he led RAND's analytic effort in support of the New American Schools Development Corporation, and he is now writing a book on lessons learned from that program. He has also examined potential national and federal policies in support of the use of technology in elementary and secondary education. He is a co-author of books on the management of research and development and the use of social experiments in policy planning. Dr. Glennan served as Director of Research and Acting Assistant Director of the Office of Economic Opportunity for Planning, Research and Evaluation before becoming the first director of the National Institute of Education in 1972.

ARTHUR C. GRAESSER is a full professor in the Department of Psychology and an adjunct professor in Mathematical Sciences at the University of Memphis. He is currently co-director of the Institute for Intelligent Systems and director of the Center for Applied Psychological Research. In 1977, Dr. Graesser received his Ph.D. in psychology from the University of California, San Diego. Dr. Graesser's primary research interests are in cognitive science and discourse processing. More specific interests include knowledge representation, question asking and answering, tutoring, text comprehension, inference generation, conversation, reading, education, memory, expert systems, artificial intelligence, and human-computer interaction. His primary interest in reading focuses on deeper levels of comprehension, such as inference generation, questioning, summarization, rhetorical organization, and pragmatics. He is currently editor of the journal *Discourse Processes* and is on the editorial board of the *Journal of Educational Psychology*, the *Journal of the Scientific Studies of Reading, Cognition & Instruction, Applied Cognitive Psychology, Poetics*, and the *International Journal of Speech Technologies*. In addition to publishing more than 200 articles in journals and books, he has written two books and has edited six.

JOHN GUTHRIE is a professor of human development at the University of Maryland at College Park. He received his Ph.D. from the University of Illinois in educational psychology. From 1992 to 1997, he was co-director of the National Reading Research Center, which conducted studies of skilled reading, writing, and knowledge development. His current research addresses cognitive and motivational processes in learning conceptual knowledge from text among elementary students. From this work, he developed an engagement model of classroom context, processes of engagement in reading, and reading outcomes. From the model, he developed Concept-Oriented Reading Instruction and conducted quasi-experiments showing that this intervention increases reading comprehension, reading motivation, and science knowledge. He has performed structural equation modeling to show that reading engagement (e.g., cognition and motivation) mediated the effects of instruction on reading strategies and knowledge outcomes. His studies are published in peer-reviewed research journals. He currently holds two grants from the National Center for Education Statistics for secondary analyses of NAEP data examining reading instructional effects on reading achievement. He served on the expert panel for the Reading Excellence Act, 1999–2000. He was a member of one National Reading Council (NRC) committee that monitored the development of the Voluntary National Tests and a second NRC committee that conducted a study of common metrics for reading achievement in 1998–2000.

MICHAEL L. KAMIL is a professor of education at Stanford University. He is a member of the Psychological Studies in Education Committee and is on the faculty of the Learning, Design, and Technology Program. His research explores the effects of a variety of technologies on literacy and the acquisition of literacy in both first and second languages. He has worked extensively in schools, reading clinics, and other learning environments to determine the appropriate balance between applications of technology and the demands of literacy. One current line of research involves a comparison of processes used by adults in reading hypertext and conventional texts. This work is being extended to similar work with young children. He is also conducting instructional research focusing on the uses of expository text for reading instruction in first and second grade. The results suggest a benefit over other instructional methods that are based almost exclusively on story or narrative text. He is a co-editor of the *Handbook of Reading Research*, Volumes I, II, and III, and has been editor of *Reading Research Quarterly* and the *Journal of Reading Behavior*. For the past two years, he has been a member of the National Reading Panel, producing a synthesis of instructional research in reading. He chaired the National Reading Panel subgroups working on comprehension, technology, and teacher education.

WILLIAM NAGY received his Ph.D. in linguistics from the University of California, San Diego. He spent a number of years at the Center for the Study of Reading at the University of Illinois, Urbana-Champaign, and is currently a professor of education at Seattle Pacific University, where he teaches graduate courses in reading. His interests include vocabulary acquisition and instruction, the role of vocabulary knowledge in first- and second-language reading, and the contributions of metalinguistic awareness to learning to read. His research has focused primarily on incidental word learning from context during reading, bilingual students' recognition of cognate relationships between English and Spanish, the acquisition of English derivational morphology and the role of morphology in word learning and reading comprehension, and the role of morphological awareness in the literacy development of children learning to read in China. He recently contributed a chapter on vocabulary acquisition processes to Volume III of the *Handbook of Reading Research*.

ANNEMARIE SULLIVAN PALINCSAR is the Jean and Charles Walgreen Jr. Chair of Literacy, associate dean for Graduate Affairs, and a teacher educator at the University of Michigan in the Educational Studies Department. Her research has focused on the design of learning environments that support self-regulation in learning activity, especially for children who experience difficulty learning in school. Her initial research (with A. Brown) was the design and investigation of reciprocal teaching dialogues to enhance reading comprehension with middle school students. Subsequent research focused on using this instruction to introduce primary-grade children to comprehension monitoring as they were learning to read. With co-principal investigator C. S. Englert, she conducted four years of research, working with special educators, to design literacy curricula and instruction that would engage special education students in using oral, written, and print literacy to accelerate their literacy learning. In her current research, conducted with science educator S. J. Magnusson, she studies how children use literacy in the context of guided inquiry science instruction, what types of text support children's inquiry, and what support students who are identified as atypical learners require to be successful in this instruction. She served as a member of the NRC's Council on the Prevention of Reading Difficulty in Young Children, the National Education Goals Panel, the Schooling Task Force of the MacArthur Pathways Project, and the National Advisory Board to the Children's Television Workshop.

GINA SCHUYLER received an M.A. in teaching from Trinity College, a B.S. in policy and management from Carnegie Mellon University, and a B.S. in history and policy from Carnegie Mellon University. She is a project coordinator for RAND Education in the Washington office. Her primary interests lie in K–12 education reform, at-risk students, and teacher quality. Her current projects include an evaluation of The Ford Foundation's Collaborating for Educational Reform Initiative, a study of 10-year strategies for programs of research for the Department of Education's Office of Educational Research and Improvement, and continuing work on an evaluation of New American Schools. Ms. Schuyler has also taught kindergarten and first grade in Washington, D.C.

DOROTHY S. STRICKLAND is the State of New Jersey Professor of Reading at Rutgers University. Her research and practice interests include early literacy learning and teaching in classrooms from preschool through the middle school years, early intervention policy and practice from pre-kindergarten through grade 3, focused intervention at the upper elementary and middle school levels, and the special needs of low-achieving poor and minority children. Current activities related to the work of the Rand Reading Study Group include membership on several teacher standards boards: the National Board for Professional Teaching Standards, the Middle Childhood/Generalist Committee; the ETS/Praxis Reading National Advisory Committee; and the INTASC/Council of State School Officers Panel on Reading. She was a panel member for the report *Preventing Reading Difficulties in Young Children* and is now working on a funded project with Dr. Catherine Snow to articulate teacher standards from pre-kindergarten through grade 4 with the design and implementation of appropriate and consistent teacher education. Relevant publications include *The Administration and Supervision of Reading Programs; Emerging Literacy: Young Children Learn to Read and Write; Language, Literacy, and the Child; Teaching Phonics Today;* and three chapters in press on classroom intervention for low-achieving students, one of which focuses on low-performing African-American children.

ANNE P. SWEET, currently scholar-in-residence at RAND, is also with the Office of Educational Research and Improvement (OERI), U.S. Department of Education, where she focuses on research in reading and K–12 literacy. She received her Ed.D. from the University of Virginia in clinical reading. As federal project officer for the Center for the Improvement of Early Reading Achievement (CIERA), she oversees field efforts to conduct research with an aim toward improving practice. She also conducts intramural research on literacy-related issues. Additionally, she works on interagency research initiatives with the National Science Foundation and the National Institute for Child Health and Human Development. Prior to joining OERI's Achievement Institute where she directs a unit on teaching and learning, she was director of the Learning and Instruction Division in OERI's Office of Research and director for Learning and Development in the National Institute of Education's Program on Teaching and Learning. Preceding her tenure with the U.S. Department of Education, Dr. Sweet was Associate Superintendent for Instruction in Virginia. Her research interests include cognitive and motivational aspects of reading achievement. She has taught reading and language arts, elementary through graduate school, and has served in various posts in public school administration and supervision. Dr. Sweet has edited a book, *Reading Research into the Year 2000;* authored book chapters; and has had articles appear in peer-reviewed research journals, most recently in the *Journal of Educational Psychology* (1998).

P. MICHAEL TIMPANE received his M.A. in history from Catholic University and his master's in public administration from Harvard University. He is RAND's senior advisor for education policy. His assignments span the range of education policy, from pre-kindergarten to postgraduate studies, and emphasize the relationships among education and other realms of social and economic policy. Currently, he is leading RAND analyses of education vouchers and of the quality standards in educational research. As vice president and senior scholar at the Carnegie Foundation for the Advancement of Teaching, prior to joining RAND, he was involved in developing all aspects of the foundation's program and in his own research assessing the progress and problems of contemporary national education reform. He is a professor of education and a former president of Teachers College, Columbia University, and has served as dean of Teachers College and deputy director and director of the federal government's National Institute of Education. He conducted research on educational policy at the Brookings Institution and at RAND in the 1970s; has served as director of Education Policy Planning for the Department of Health, Education and Welfare; and has worked in the Department of Defense as a historian for the Joint Chiefs of Staff and as a special assistant for civil rights in the Office of the Assistant Secretary of Defense (Manpower). He has published numerous articles on education policy and has edited and contributed to several books on education and social policy. He has, for more than two decades, helped direct the Aspen Institute's Program for Education in a Changing Society. Through this, and as advisor to state and federal policymakers, he has participated in the development of new perspectives on national goals and standards in education, comprehensive services for young children, higher education, youth policy, education and work, learning and technology, and the democratic purposes of schooling. Internationally, he has represented the United States in missions to the Organization for Economic Cooperation and Development, India, Iran, Israel, and the People's Republic of China, and has served as a visiting fellow for the Fulbright Commission in Italy, Austria, and Portugal and has served as a Japan Society leadership fellow in Tokyo. He is a member of the Pew Forum on Education Reform, for which he recently organized and edited a volume of essays on higher education's involvement in precollegiate school reform. He serves on boards of the Children's Television Workshop, the Southern Education Foundation, and Jobs for the Future and on the visiting committee of the Harvard Graduate School of Education. He has also served on the boards of the American Council on Education and the American Association of Higher Education. He has received honorary doctorates from Wagner College and Catholic University.

FRANK R. VELLUTINO is a professor of psychology at the State University of New York at Albany. He currently holds joint faculty appointments in the Department of Psychology (Cognitive Psychology Program), the Department of Educational and Counseling Psychology, and the Program in Linguistics and Cognitive Science of the Department of Anthropology. He is also director of the Child Research and Study Center, a research and student training center. He currently teaches a graduate course in children's learning that emphasizes intellectual, perceptual, memory, and language development, as well as a graduate seminar in human development that focuses on the relationship between language and cognitive development. His research has been concerned with the cognitive underpinnings of reading development as well as the relationship between reading difficulties and various aspects of language and other cognitive functions. His research has generated numerous articles in refereed journals, in addition to a book and numerous book chapters addressing the causes and correlates of reading difficulties in young children. Dr. Vellutino's most recent research seeks to develop models of early intervention that effectively reduce the number of children who continue to have long-term reading difficulties and, thereby, further our understanding of reading development.

JOANNA WILLIAMS is a professor of psychology and education at Teachers College, Columbia University. Her research interests include the processes involved in beginning reading and in comprehension and reading instruction for students with learning disabilities and other students at risk for school failure. In the late 1970s, Dr. Williams developed a program to teach phonemic awareness to students with learning disabilities (*The ABDs of Reading*). Her work has explored differences in the comprehension patterns of normally developing students and students with learning disabilities, and she has demonstrated a link between the editing difficulties during listening and reading (inability to inhibit competing associations) of students with learning disabilities and their comprehension performance. Recently she developed a program, The Theme Scheme, that helps children go beyond plot-level comprehension to a more abstract understanding of story themes and how they relate to real-life experiences. Dr. Williams has also been active in training and curriculum development projects related to the professional development of teachers. She was editor of the *Journal of Educational Psychology* from 1973 to 1978, and she is the founding editor of *Scientific Studies of Reading* (1997–present). She was a member of the National Reading Panel.